Sociology Tomorrow

PETER PARK

Sociology
Tomorrow

PEGASUS • NEW YORK

Library of Congress Catalog Card Number 68-27989

TO MY MOTHER

PREFACE

THE OBSCURE and remote origins of this essay undoubtedly go back to my student days, perhaps to my infancy. I shall not attempt to trace these here. The more specific and recent impetus to it, however, can be pinpointed without equivocation. Peter d'A. Jones, my friend and the editor of this book asked me to sum up and examine, for the benefit of the general reading public, what modern sociologists are up to. This invitation, which I accepted as a challenge, about two years ago, not only was the beginning of this essay but was to set the tone for it as well. The idea of writing for the general public, rather than for other sociologists, was intriguing, for it meant that the more commonly accepted notions and methods of the sociological fraternity could not be taken for granted; that is, it offered an opportunity to examine the more basic aspects of modern sociology. As the essay began to take shape, this aspect was to loom larger than I initially envisioned, and the end product is more a critique than a review. This may not be exactly what my editor had ordered, but he was gracious enough to accept it as it is.

The "general reader," to whom this book is supposed to be addressed, is partly responsible for its style. But I have had trouble fixing his image in my mind: he has been, in turn, a sophomore, a professor of English, a housewife, a photographer, an anti-science graduate student of sociology, and many others who have been flashed on and off my mental screen. This, more than the variation in the subject matter, explains any unevenness in the pace and the density of the discussion. Initially, anyway, the readers of this book were not supposed to have been, to any significant extent, my fellow sociologists, a consideration accounting for the no-footnote policy adopted at the outset and adhered to throughout. But as I began to get deeper into the roots of modern sociological practices, I found sociologists claiming an increasingly larger share of my attention, with the unfortunate consequence that passages thickened with references to materials not within the purview of the general reader. These sections will be thought too technical by some, not technical enough by others. My apologies to both, especially to those who will deplore the lack of reference citations; it was with some effort that I restrained my school-conditioned hand from reaching out to insert documenting footnotes in these passages. Despite this split in focus, I hope the book will be read, with some benefit, by those who wonder about the present state of sociology and its possible future—that is, by exploring students, established professionals, and interested general readers who are often confused by sociologists.

Numerous hands have taken part in the shaping of this essay into a book. Peter Jones worked unstintingly to improve the presentation, as only a friend could have. Kate Roby was helpful in simplifying and strengthening the language of the essay. I have benefited enormously from the thoughtful comments of Milton Gordon, Beau Fly Jones, Murray Kiteley, Henry Korson, Charles Page, Albert Pierce, Tote Roby, and Barry Wax, who spared me from the more careless errors of omission and commission and gave me encouragement even as they disagreed with some of my stubborn contentions. Many of the ideas expressed in this book were conceived, born, and nurtured during seminar discussions with graduate students at the University of Massachusetts (Amherst), who must be acknowledged here, if only collectively and anonymously, as indirect but important contributors to this book. The discussions that I had with my colleagues and students while I was committing my thoughts to paper have been especially helpful. I was materially aided by the Department of Sociology and Anthropology of the University of Massachusetts in the preparation of the first typescript. I have been fortunate in the able services of Janet Kitterly and Elizabeth Howorth, who typed the drafts. I reserve a special mention for my wife, whose role in the creation of this book has been intimate and pervasive; she partook in it with support, advice, and help, bearing with cheerfulness the more unpleasant by-products of what has become a drawn-out process. My thanks to all.

PETER PARK

Rome, 1969

CONTENTS

INTRODUCTION

Sociology, since the word was coined by August Comte in 1839, has been thought of as a science, at least by most sociologists. There is no compelling reason why sociology should be a science, no more than why mountain climbing should be one. But the fact is that today in sociology even those who think of themselves as latter-day soothsayers ministering to an entire society refer to themselves, perhaps in slips of the tongue, as social scientists. This practice at least partially betrays attempts on the part of sociologists to partake of the honor bestowed upon science, much as does Mrs. Eddy's calling her religion Christian Science. But more basically it stems from a misunderstanding of the limitations as well as the requirements of science itself.

Sociology is supposed to promote understanding of social phenomena. Leaving aside the practical aspect, science too imparts understanding, an understanding of nature. But not all understanding is therefore science. Much insight into human behavior and the world we live in can be gained by reading a good novel or a creative history, but it would be silly to subsume literature or history under science merely because they are illuminating and because science is the valued mode of knowledge today. The totality of human sensibility is bigger than science, for science relates only to selected aspects of nature. To Newton the falling apple was merely a body obeying the law of universal gravitation which it occasioned to be discovered, not a piece of fruit to be appreciated for its appearance or taste. Science is a way of knowledge that has its own demands and limits, and whether or not one pursues it, in the final analysis, is a matter of personal temperament.

There is much value, of course, in talking about society in terms other than those of science. A sociologist may thus choose to criticize, preach, or philosophize about social issues. These activities, however, though useful, should not be confused with science. It is perhaps in the interest of both the scientific and the nonscientific elements in sociology to make this distinction, for confounding art and science, or philosophy and science, for that matter, does not contribute to either. Had Newton been an apple fancier, the history of science might have turned out rather differently. The nonscientific aspects of sociology, much as they are appreciated, are not in the purview of this essay, and I will have no more to say about them.

Sociology has been singularly unproductive as a science; it may be said fairly that there is not a quantitative generalization in sociology that can claim universal, or near universal, validity. This is in spite of the apparent fact that sociology today is a complex edifice made up of theories, deductions, hypotheses, instruments, measurements, and, sometimes, mathematics. Something seems to have gone wrong with science as applied to social phenomena.

Sociologists have tended to learn about science second- or third-hand from philosophers of science, whose job is to analyze the logical structure of science as a finished product. As a consequence, they have gained a two-dimensional and upside-down view of science. Had sociologists had direct contact with the physical sciences, especially from an historical point of view— that is, in terms of how they began and how they changed—they might have invested their energy in an aspect of science-building other than the formal and technical apparatus, perhaps with a more fruitful result. This aspect is the *conceptual foundation* of science, an ironic thing for sociologists, of all people, to overlook.

Analogies for sociology have been drawn from various branches and stages of science, such as Newtonian mechanics, astronomy before Copernicus, chemistry at the time of the construction of Mendeleev's periodic table of elements, biological Darwinism, and even, in dizzy moments, quantum mechanics. There is perhaps an element of truth in each of these suggestive analogies. But, really, sociology today is in a pre-scientific state, corresponding to the stage of scientific development that physics was in before Galileo. There is much in current sociology that resembles the Aristotelian physics of this period. If, therefore, a lesson is to be drawn from science, it must be from the Galilean revolution, for this was the beginning of modern science, not just physics, but all of it. This revolution was premised on a fundamental change in the commonly accepted conceptual mold. The ripples from this original quake have been reaching the other shores of science, one by one, but have not yet touched sociology.

The purpose of this essay is, then, to examine current sociological practices, both theories and methods, and discover the conceptual elements that need to be turned around or eradicated before sociology can function as a science. The discussion begins with what science does and how it emerged from the larval stages, which find obvious analogies in sociology today. It will be seen that the conceptual heritage that stands in the way of revolutionizing sociology as a science manifests itself both in its main theories and in the established methods of testing them, in which measurement plays a crucial role.

There still remains the possibility that the failure of sociology to produce tangible and satisfying results as a science is due to the inherent impossibility of applying science to social phenomena, no matter how much the scope of the application is to be restricted. No attempt will be made here to argue against this assumption, for in the final analysis it can best be proven false by producing a successful science of sociology. The following analysis of why sociology has not emerged as a viable science is intended as a step toward making science possible in sociology.

Science

This section is devoted to a discussion of science, which is to serve as a framework for the critique of modern sociology to follow. It implicitly views science as an intellectual activity that produces *a kind of* understanding of the world we confront—not necessarily *the* or *the best kind of* understanding, but just *a* kind that suits a personal temperament which insists on backing up speculation with demonstration. The explanatory aspect of science consequently occupies, at least initially, a central position in the discussion, and the deductive nature of scientific explanation is duly noted. But what distinguishes a scientific explanation from other kinds is not so much the deductive nature of the explanation as where the deductions come from and where they lead, that is, the conceptual foundation and the empirical end of the explanation. Our discussion accordingly will focus on these latter points, opposing science to common sense, and showing how the Scientific Revolution liberated medieval science from the constraints of common sense. Since a fuller analysis of defects in existing sociological explanations will occupy the rest of the book, in this section current sociological practices are brought in sparingly, as occasional counterpoints to the main theme.

I. Scientific Explanation: A Kind of Understanding

MUCH of the power and attraction that science exerts derives from its ability to explain the events it deals with. Science has enabled man to control his environment, at times with spectacular success, because it equips him with a kind of understanding of the world that can be directly translated into tangible results. To be sure, science does not have a monopoly on explanation. Explanations of one kind or another are constantly proferred by the man in the street without the benefit of science, and a common sense explanation, too, imparts understanding of sorts. Science, after all, has its beginning in common sense, and there are rudimentary similarities in the logical structure between common sense explanation and the scientific variety. The latter, however, stands apart from the former in its persistent adherence to explicit and systematic rules of reasoning and operation.

Sociology explains human events: the rise of capitalism, the fact of social inequality, social disorganization, etc. The logical structure of sociological explanation, as will be seen in detail later on (Chapters VI, VII, and VIII), shares something in common with explanations in the physical sciences. But since this structure is discernible, however attenuated, in common sense explanations as well, the claim of today's sociology to a scientific status cannot rest on formal characteristics of explanation. In fact, *sociology, in its more crucial aspects, is much closer to common sense than to science.* These aspects have to do with checking the validity of an explanation against available facts, and drawing tangible consequences from the explanation for practical ends. These two facets of scientific explanation are intimately related to each other, as will be shown in the following pages (especially Chapters III and IV), and together they make science the potent intellectual activity that it is. The deficiencies of sociology as a science must therefore be looked for, not in the *logical* structure of sociological explanation, but in other aspects of sociology as practiced today.

Let us first look at a simple illustrative example of scientific explanation. How does science explain the fact that water boils at a lower temperature on a mountain than at the seashore? It may be explained briefly that the air surrounding the earth exerts atmospheric pressure on any surface, except when it is enclosed in a vacuum, and water boils at a different temperature depending on the magnitude of the pressure applied on it—the relationship being that the lower the pressure, the lower the temperature at which water boils. Since the atmospheric pressure is lower on a mountain than at the seashore, water boils at a lower temperature there. Schematically, the general fact that water boils at a lower temperature on a mountain top than at the seashore follows from two other generalities: one, that the atmospheric pressure decreases as one rises in the atmosphere; and, two, that the temperature at which water boils (boiling point) decreases as the pressure decreases. Logically, then, when the statement concerning the fact to be explained is deduced from statements of a general nature, we say that the fact is explained. At least, this is the skeletal structure of explanation in science; but most, if not all, of what passes for an explanation in everyday discourse probably can also be shown to have this logical structure.

Take, for example, a common sense explanation of the high suicide rate in Sweden in comparison with that of the United States. It is alleged that a welfare state robs a person of initiative and, by implication, a loss of initiative leads to suicide. From this, and the fact that Sweden is a prime example of the welfare state, while the United States is the land of private enterprise, it follows that the suicide rate is higher in Sweden.

Here again the statement concerning the fact to be explained, namely the high rate of suicide in Sweden, is logically deducible from two statements of a general nature—one, that welfare states rob a person of initiative, and two, that a loss of initiative leads to suicide, provided that it is understood that Sweden is a welfare state. The logical structure of this explanation is identical with that of boiling water, except for the fact that in this instance an additional step is needed in the deductive chain to establish that Sweden is a welfare state. This is necessary because the fact to be explained here is a concrete, historical event, whereas in the case of boiling water it is a general phenomenon—that water boils faster at a higher altitude. To explain the fact that water boils faster in Mexico City than in Boston, it would similarly be necessary to equate high and low altitudes with Mexico City and Boston, respectively.

The fact that the suicide rate varies from country to country was given a sociological explanation half a century ago in a classic treatise, *Suicide*, by a celebrated sociologist Emile Durkheim (1858–1917). Using the statistics, in the main, of the nineteenth century, he observed that Catholic countries in general have lower suicide rates than Protestant ones. He explained this phenomenon by postulating (1) "a religious society cannot exist without a collective *credo* and the more extensive the credo the more unified and strong is the society"; (2) the more a society is unified or integrated, the more resistant its members to suicide. From these assertions, plus the observation that Protestantism is rent by doctrinal schisms, it follows, loosely speaking, that Protestant countries have higher suicide rates than Catholic ones. The structural similarity of this explanation to the examples taken above from science and common sense is evident.

To say that explanations have the same logical structure is, of course, not to say that they are the same in other respects as well. In science what is offered as an explanation of an event or phenomenon must be squared with observable facts. The business of squaring an explanation with facts—what philosophers of science often refer to as empirical verification or confirmation—is not a simple matter and sometimes requires arduous effort of both a mental and physical nature. What is accepted as a common sense explanation, by contrast, is not usually held up against facts to see if it is valid, and, even when it is, the language of explanation may be such that it is difficult to determine its validity. In the common sense explanation of suicide, for example, a quick check of available statistics would have shown that Norway, a welfare state, has a relatively low rate of suicide, and Austria, a nonwelfare state, has a high one—facts that would have placed the explanation in a dubious light. But this is not as blatant a disregard of facts on the part of common sense as it may seem, because of extenuating circumstances. For one thing, it is uncertain what is meant by welfare state, that is, whether Norway is in some sense less of a welfare state than Sweden, and Austria a kind of hidden welfare state. For another thing, it is not clear, the way the explanation is framed, whether factors other than welfarism lead to a high suicide rate. And last, it is not specified what is meant by a high suicide rate. Besides, the so-called "facts" themselves have rather tenuous status. The practice of keeping official statistics on suicide varies from state to state, and the attitude of the people toward suicide itself is different in various societies, so that suicide may not be reported with uniform conscientiousness in all countries. These ambiguities are rather typical accompaniments of common sense explanations.

Similar difficulties plague sociological explanations, though perhaps in ways more complicated and less obvious. In the explanation of suicide, it is evident enough that there is a greater diversity of beliefs among Protestants than Catholics, as it is easily ascertainable that the suicide rate is, by and large, higher in Protestant countries than in Catholic ones. But it is by no means clear if diversity of beliefs necessarily entails social disunity (disintegration). Indeed, it is not certain if disunity (disintegration) means anything other than diversity of beliefs itself, in view of the fact that the former is an abstract idea whose concrete manifestations are not pinpointed. Under the circumstances, Durkheim's explanation of suicide has the danger of being true by definition and hence of being not empirically verifiable. Attempts have been made, of course, to render aspects of Durkheim's explanation more amenable to empirical test in recent years, but his central ideas still remain elusive in scientific terms, as will be seen in Chapter XI. This is also true of the key notions in other sociological explanations. But I am running ahead of myself here, for the burden of this whole essay is to show the impasse to which sociology has been brought by its explanatory concepts. For now, let us return to the explanation of boiling water to see how an explanation is tested in science.

It can be easily demonstrated that the explanation of boiling water agrees with facts which are readily verifiable. A logical consequence of the explanation is that water should boil in New York at about the same temperature as in Boston, at a lower temperature in Mexico City (7,700 ft.), and a still lower temperature in La Paz, Bolivia (11,909 ft.). Indeed, it can be shown that water in an open pan boils at approximately 100 degrees centigrade (100° C., 212° F.) in New York as in Boston, at about 93 degrees centigrade (93° C., 199° F.) in Mexico City, and at about 88 degrees centigrade (88° C., 190° F.) in La Paz. This fact, however, does not demonstrate that the two general statements in the explanation are true; it is only indirect and partial evidence that the explanation is not contradicted by facts. The general statements in question can also be tested against facts more directly, however. In this day and age, it can be shown to the satisfaction of all but the most skeptical that the barometric pressure is higher on the ground than on a mountain and that it drops as the altitude increases. It can also be shown in a high school laboratory that the boiling point of water varies directly (though not necessarily proportionately) with pressure. The experiment would consist of water contained in a vessel, the internal pressure of which can be varied by partially evacuating or compressing air with a vacuum pump. With suitable temperature and pressure gauges attached to this vessel, the boiling point of water can be read under different pressures. This experiment would show that the boiling point of water indeed varies inversely with pressure, within a moderate range of pressure.

One of the things which makes these experiments meaningful as a test of the explanation is the high degree of general agreement among people, not just scientists, as to when a body of water is said to be boiling. To be sure, there will be some disagreement about exactly when water begins to boil, and for this reason in more refined scientific studies boiling needs to be defined more precisely than, say, by formation and bursting of bubbles. But for the kind of crude experiment needed to demonstrate the validity of the explanation in general terms, the everyday criterion of boiling is perhaps sufficiently unambiguous. Another necessary element is our acceptance of the pressure and temperature gauges used in these experiments. The use of these instruments has become so commonplace that we take it for granted that a barometer measures air pressure and a thermometer, temperature. The workings of these instruments, of course, do not have to be taken on faith; it can be shown with a little demonstration that they are as sensibly valid as a beam balance is for weighing bodies. But to the extent that these instruments are accepted as measures of pressure and temperature, we can agree on the meaning of the experiments without delving into the logical status of the instruments used.

It is a truism that sociological concepts, as well as common sense ones, are imprecisely defined and that there is little agreement in the way they are understood and measured. It will be argued in this essay that the reasons for the lack of precision and agreement in sociology are in the nature of the concepts themselves, which are too far removed from objective referents to be useful in the context of empirical verification. No amount of verbal analysis ("theoretical" discussion) will therefore really make existing sociological explanations more empirically accountable. Nor will the development of new "measuring instruments" necessarily produce agreement among sociologists as long as sociological concepts are thought of as Platonic ideas only the shadows of which are measured. The meaning of objectivity in science is that its fundamental concepts are grounded in common practices of men, and it is this objectivity which gives science its measuring instruments, its precise concepts, and, in the final analysis, its empirically verifiable explanations. Quantification, a key element in the development of modern science, derives from the same source, to anticipate the discussion of Chapter IX. The absence of this "grass root" foundation in sociology makes it difficult to square explanations with empirical facts.

The point of juxtaposing a common sense explanation, or a sociological one, with a scientific explanation in this manner is not that one is always demonstrably true and the other always false. The history of science is dotted with explanations that we now know to be false but were adjudged to be satisfactory by scientists of bygone days. The celebrated case of phlogiston theory is a good example. Before the advent of modern chemistry it was held that when a combustible substance, such as charcoal, is burned, phlogiston is liberated and it mixes with air or other available substances nearby. This, scientists maintained, accounted for the process of winning metals from ores. It was explained that when iron ore is heated in burning coal, the phlogiston escaping from the coal combines with the ore to form a metal. The same principle was thought to underly the fact that vitriolic acid (what we now call sulfuric acid) is obtained by burning sulfur, only in this case the phlogiston liberated by the burning of sulfur is given to the air. This theory of phlogiston was eventually thrown out with the discovery of oxygen and the understanding of oxidation. But for about a hundred years, roughly during the eighteenth century, it was considered a satisfactory explanation accounting for diverse experiences of metallurgists in their shops and chemists in their laboratories. It was the only theory that could serve this purpose at the time. Nor are common sense explanations always demonstrably wrong. The commonly held view that unhappiness causes suicide may or may not be illuminating of human behavior, but certainly it

is a difficult statement to refute empirically, for the reasons
which will become clearer in the course of this essay (see Chapter V). Hence its tenacity. From a scientific point of view, a
theory that is empirically not testable is worse than one that can
be demonstrated to be false.

The point is rather that science insists on objective evidence
whereas common sense is somewhat lackadaisical about verification of the explanations it advances. And it is this insistence
which sets the style of scientific discourse, shapes its content,
guides scientists' activities, and produces a kind of understanding of the world with momentous practical consequences not
possible without science. In sociology, the verificational requirements of science are officially recognized, but a prevailing
mystique of understanding, as will be seen in later sections, has
prevented them from being fully satisfied. *The result is an
aborted science.*

II. Theory:
An Example

THE EXPLANATION of the variation in the boiling point of water given in the preceding chapter is not complete. It raises further questions: "Why does the atmospheric pressure decrease with altitude?" "Why does water boil at a lower temperature under a lower pressure?" A fuller answer to these questions calls forth statements of greater and greater generality until, ultimately, all fundamental principles of modern physical science have been invoked. What is brought forth in this process is a scientific theory. The explanations of suicide are, of course, equally incomplete, for it is reasonable to ask further: "Why does loss of initiative lead to suicide?" Or, "Why does lack of social integration cause suicide?" A typical common sense approach to such probing questions is to resort to intuitive and "self-evident" truths, such as, for example, that lack of initiative in life means no desire to live. At any rate, the language and reasoning become more speculative and less precise and thus empirical verification is rendered more difficult. Similar tendencies are evident in sociological theories, as will be documented in Chapters VI, VII, and VIII. In Durkheim's explanation of suicide, for instance, the concept of "anomie" is introduced, which is in turn linked to intuitively appealing notions such as "despair" and "will to live." But deferring to Chapter XI a fuller discussion of how "anomie" figures as an explanatory concept in modern sociology, the more important rungs in the explanatory ladder, stretching upward from the phenomenon of boiling water, can be noted here to advantage. This sketch will serve the purpose of further baring the structure of scientific explanation

25

and will be useful as a frame of reference for the discussion of sociological explanations to come later on.

The earth is wrapped in layers of air which are composed of various gases, primarily oxygen and nitrogen, and of small particles, such as dust and smoke in insignificant proportions. The air has weight and exerts pressure on the surface of the earth, as on any body it impinges on. The sea level is the bottom of the bottom layer of air engulfing the earth, where more air bears down on a unit area; this air is more compressed than in the atmosphere some distance removed from the earth. As a consequence, the atmospheric pressure decreases with altitude. This explains the relationship between altitude and atmospheric pressure. Note here that the structure of the explanation is deductive. The ready verifiability of the explaining statements is also noteworthy. Bottles of air can be weighed to show that they are heavier than comparable bottles from which air has been evacuated. The fact that air can be compressed does not require much of a demonstration. Common automobile tires are filled with compressed air—the air from a single tire can fill many balloons, the total volume of which far exceeds the volume of the tire.

The weight and the compressibility of gases can further be explained, if required, in terms of more general principles, such as the molecular composition of matter, the behavior and the atomic structure of molecules, subatomic particles, etc. This process can be continued until it reaches the very frontier of science. Along the way, empirical verification becomes increasingly less a matter of statement-by-statement check against fact. Already at the level where references are made to molecules, the characteristics and the behavior of molecules cannot be directly observed, and any statement concerning these matters are verified only indirectly and by inferential evidence. The system of concepts, such as molecules and atoms, and assumptions concerning their characteristics and behavior that serve to explain a large body of observational data is referred to as a theory. Although the fundamental notions of a theory are not directly sensible, the consequences deduced from it must be empirically verifiable for it to be accepted as a scientific theory. In this sense it is more than mere speculation, although it contains speculative elements.

To give an example of a successful scientific theory which illustrates the importance of speculative concepts, let us pursue the explanation of the relationship between the boiling point of water and pressure. What follows is a thumbnail sketch of the kinetic theory of matter, a showcase of physical science. In this theory, matter is supposed to be composed of submicroscopic particles called molecules. Chemically distinguishable substances (i.e., substances that have different chemical reactions) are composed of different kinds of molecules. Water for instance, is made up of one kind of molecule and common salt of another kind. When molecules are packed tightly under pressure, the outward characteristics of the substance they make up are different from when the molecules are more loosely assembled. A substance manifests itself in three different phases depending on how closely its molecules are pressed together—solid, liquid, and gas. Ice, water, and vapor, for example, represent the three phases of a substance resulting from progressively looser arrangements of its molecules.

It is further assumed that molecules are in continual motion, whether flying from one point to another (translational) or turning around their own axes (rotational). In the gaseous state, the molecules dash about almost independently of one another, but in the liquid state they are held together, like dance partners, by a force of mutual attraction, resulting from their proximity to one another, and consequently their (translational) movement is more restricted. This force of attraction is assumed to be negligible in the gaseous state, since the molecules are separated by immense space in comparison with their tiny size. In the solid state, however, this force exerts such a powerful restraint on the molecules that they merely vibrate around fixed points. This explains the amorphousness of gases, the fluidity of liquids, and the rigidity of solids.

A quantitative concept associated with a body in motion is kinetic energy, symbolized by E_k. It is defined as one-half mass (m) times velocity (v) squared ($E_k = mv^2/2$). For our purpose, the mass of a body can be represented by its weight and the velocity by its speed of motion. Thus, the more a body weighs and the faster it moves, the greater its kinetic energy. In this theory heat is thought of as a form of kinetic energy such that what is commonly referred to as heating an object is a process of increasing the kinetic energy of its constituent molecules. And, naturally enough, the (absolute) temperature of an object is assumed to be proportional to the average kinetic energy of the molecules in the object. (A more quantitative rendition of the kinetic theory is to be found in Chapter XII.)

Although the molecules of a liquid at a certain temperature have a certain average kinetic energy, there is expected to be some variation in the kinetic energy of the individual molecules, some possessing more and some less. The more energetic of the liquid molecules manage to loosen themselves from the others with which they are bonded together in the liquid state and escape into the space above the surface of the liquid; that is, they become gas molecules and move about more freely. This process is known as evaporation, and it is accompanied by a drop in the temperature because the molecules in tearing themselves away from the pull of the other molecules lose some of their kinetic energy. If evaporation takes place in a closed container, the free space above the liquid becomes progressively more crowded with liberated molecules, which keep on jostling. In the course of dashing about, some of these liberated molecules are bound to hit the surface of the liquid, as well as the inner walls of the container, and get trapped back into bondage with the other liquid molecules; that is, they return to the liquid state. This process is known as condensation, and it is accompanied by a gain in the temperature of the liquid because of the increase in the kinetic energy of the molecules due to the molecular attraction. Now, equate the per unit area momentum of the gas molecules bombarding the inner walls of the container and the surface of the liquid with the pressure of the gas in the space above the liquid, the momentum of a molecule (M) being equal to mass times velocity (M = mv). It then follows that the more crowded the space becomes with gas molecules and the faster each molecule moves around, the greater the pressure becomes in the area, and the rate of condensation increases. And when the pressure reaches a certain point at a given temperature, the rate of condensation matches that of evaporation, and a state of equilibrium is reached. What is commonly referred to as the boiling point represents such a state of equilibrium. Incidentally, at this equilibrium point the temperature of the liquid remains constant, since evaporation is balanced by condensation. It is for this reason that boiling water at sea level remains at 100° C. At a low temperature the rate of evaporation is low because the average kinetic energy of the molecules is small, and hence only a low pressure is required to attain the point of equilibrium. But at a higher temperature, the rate of evaporation increases, and the equilibrium is reached at a correspondingly higher pressure.

Now, when water is heated in an open pan, the pressure in the space above the water is that of the atmosphere, and the water has to be heated until it reaches the temperature at which the rate of evaporation matches the rate of condensation at that pressure. At sea level, for example, the atmospheric pressure is 760 mm. (37.7 in.) on the barometer, and water boils at 100° C. (212° F.); at an altitude of 4,500 feet above sea level, the atmospheric pressure is 644 mm. (25.4 in.) and water boils at 95.4° C. (203.7° F.).

This theory contains assumptions that cannot be verified, as the concept of molecules itself is a hypothetical construct not subject to direct observation. The assumptions are: that molecules are in constant motion; that they exert attractive force on one another in the liquid state; that they fly in a straight line in the gaseous state; that their momentum gives rise to the pressure of gas on the walls of the container; and, that the temperature is proportional to the average kinetic energy of the molecules. It renders the more familiar natural phenomena, such as

boiling, condensation, and evaporation, in terms of the hypothetical behavior of molecules. It may seem like a rather elaborate
edifice to explain a simple phenomenon of water boiling at
different temperatures under different pressures. It may even
seem farfetched. But its validity—and its beauty—lies in its ability to account for a host of other observable phenomena, especially the behavior of gases. The fact that water boiling in an
open pan remains at 100° C. at sea level, which was brought out
rather gratuitously in the course of developing the explanation
above, is such a phenomenon.

The well-established chemical principle that the product of
the volume and the pressure of a sample of a gas remains constant at a constant temperature ($PV =$ constant), provided that
the density of the gas is not too high and the temperature not
too low, which is one form of what is known as Boyle's Law,
can also be easily deduced from the kinetic theory of gas. When
the volume of the vessel containing a gas is reduced, say, to
one-half the initial volume, keeping the temperature constant,
the walls of the vessel get bombarded by the molecules with a
frequency increased by the same proportion, namely, twice as
frequently as before. Since pressure is assumed to result from
the bombardment of the molecules, the more frequent the bombardment the greater the pressure. If the volume decreases by
one-half and the pressure doubles, the product of these two
must remain the same as before, that is, $PV =$ constant. (This
deduction can be carried out more precisely and in more detail
using the quantitative definitions of the concepts involved and
mathematical equations, as can be seen in Chapter XII, but here
this verbal argument will have to suffice.) This explanation is
made possible by bringing into play the more basic concepts of
classical physics, such as mass, velocity, force, momentum, and
pressure, although the way these contribute to the explanation is
not made explicit here. Similarly, other well-known generalities
in physical chemistry that are called laws, bearing the names of
Gay-Lussac, Charles, Dalton, Joules, and Avogadro, can be explained in terms of this theory. This circumstance partly

substantiates the soundness of the theory. It has, of course, stood up against other empirical tests as well. To cite a more interesting example, the average speeds of different molecules, which can be mathematically deduced from a quantitative version of the kinetic theory, have been shown to agree rather closely with the empirical results obtained from ingenious modern experiments.

It must not be thought for a moment that the above theory was constructed in one piece specifically to account for the behavior of water in a pan. It is a collage of physical principles that were developed over a couple of centuries, the chief ones being Newton's classical laws of physics, which have successfully been applied to the behavior of macroscopic bodies in motion. In contrast, common sense "theories" and, to a large extent, sociological ones as well, are built up from beginning to end, in an ever-spiraling edifice of abstraction, to explain a puzzling phenomenon, such as suicide. That is, the generalities which are brought in to do the explaining tend to be invented on the spur of the moment, others in turn are conjured up to cover these, and so forth. These common sense ideas are often intuitively appealing but are usually expressed in such a manner as to defy empirical test. The result is an explanation that is merely plausible.

An important characteristic of a successful scientific theory, which might be surmised from the above discussion, is that as it grows in generality the explanation it entails becomes more, rather than less, amenable to empirical accounting, a characteristic not shared by nonscientific theories. This is because the more general a theory is, the larger the number of specific empirical facts it subsumes, all of which can be brought to bear on the phenomenon to be explained. But to the extent that what passes for a theory is a loose assemblage of vague generalities, as is often the case in sociology, it does not contribute much toward establishing the validity of the explanation it advances. Before examining in detail the difficulties encountered in sociological explanations, I now turn to a general discussion of the manner in which a theory is tested in science.

III. Prediction: Testing a Theory

The ability to predict future events is regarded by sociologists as the mark of a mature science. By the same token, the failure of sociology to foresee more spectacular events in recent history, such as the eruption of rebellion in black ghettos, is dejectedly accepted as a sign of inadequacy. There is power approaching magic in being able to foretell the future, power that is enjoyed by prophets, fortune tellers, astrologers, and other types of soothsayers. To be sure, scientists also make predictions, but this fact does not make soothsaying a science. Besides, scientific prediction, unlike soothsaying, is always predicated on circumstantial factors and therefore is conditional in application. Where natural events are concerned, that is, events not created or manipulated under laboratory conditions, the factors affecting the course of events are usually not fully identified and, as a consequence, precise prediction of these events is difficult, if not impossible, even in physical sciences. There is a tendency to look upon astronomy as a model of sociology, but the success of astronomy in predicting natural events (which, as a matter of fact, precedes the advent of classical physics) is surely a singular achievement even among natural sciences. Astronomy has been in a unique position of dealing with repetitive happenings that take place in a laboratory-like setting where perturbations from the "outside" are, for all practical purposes, nonexistent. The scientific prowess to predict can be overestimated, as it can also be sought after for dubious reasons from a scientific point of view.

Prediction, whether scientific or occultist, is tantalizing and, when effective, overpowering beyond words. Prediction also figures in technological applications of science in controlling the environment and creating practical artifacts, as will be seen in the next chapter. But the central significance of prediction in science as an intellectual pursuit is that it provides a peculiarly pursuasive means of checking an explanation against facts. How satisfying, for instance, Durkheim's explanation of suicide would be if it were possible to predict that a particular country undergoing a process of social disintegration would gain in suicide rate by so many suicides per million inhabitants, and to have this prediction come true—satisfying, of course, not for the increase in the suicide rate but for the efficacy of the explanation that makes this prediction possible. That such a prediction is not possible in sociology is due, to a large extent, to the nature of the sociological phenomena, which cannot be observed and/or manipulated under laboratory conditions; it also results from an inherent weakness in the currently prevalent sociological explanations, as will be argued in later chapters (especially VI, VII, and VIII). Of course, there is an intimate, if not inevitable, relationship between the type of phenomena being explained and the type of explanations offered. In any event, in order to understand why sociology cannot produce successful predictions, the importance of prediction in the context of verification must first be grasped.

1.

The validity of an explanation initially rests on the success with which it accounts for known facts other than those which are the immediate object of the explanation. Thus the kinetic theory, which explains the relationship between pressure and the boiling point, also explains the workings of a pressure cooker. When water boils in an open pan with a loose lid on it, the vapor escapes from the water into the air, and the vapor pressure in the cooking vessel is maintained more or less at that of the room—about 760 mm. of mercury column at sea level. As long as this condition prevails, the temperature of the boiling water remains at about 100° C. If a tight lid is placed over the pan so that vapor cannot escape from it as easily, the internal vapor pressure builds up to a point above the normal atmospheric pressure, and water boils at a higher temperature. This is the reason why food cooks faster in a pressure cooker.

Predictions are crucial in establishing the validity of an explanation beyond the level of plausibility. The prediction that water should boil at a lower temperature on the top floor of the Empire State Building than on the ground floor is one that we can make confidently—because the theory from which it is derived has been tested and we normally would not even bother to ascertain it by carrying out the experiment dictated by the statement. Similarly, we have enough confidence in modern astronomy to believe that there was a lunar eclipse on March 13, 1960, even if we did not witness it ourselves, and to anticipate another one on January 30, 1972. But predictions played a rather decisive role at key points in developing modern scientific theories. It might be worthwhile to cite a couple of illustrious examples from the history of science.

It was a generally well-known fact around the time of Galileo (1564–1642) that a suction pump could not draw water from a depth greater than about 34 feet. This was a phenomenon that Galileo himself could not explain, a puzzle whose solution was left to his disciple, Torricelli (1608–1647). Torricelli somehow conceived the idea that the atmosphere is a "sea of air," and with the aid of hydrostatics, a body of knowledge concerning the behavior of liquids at rest, which had been rather well developed by this time, proceeded to explain why a suction pump cannot support a column of water longer than 34 feet in height. The pressure exerted by the weight of air on the water in which the pump is immersed, so the explanation went, pushes the water up the cylinder of the pump from which air has been evacuated by the action of the pump. The water rises in the cylinder until the water column balances the air pressure on the water surrounding the pump. That is, the air pressure suspends a column of water 34 feet long in a vacuum. From this he deduced—predicted—that mercury, which is fourteen times as heavy as water, would be similarly suspended in a vacuum by air pressure but only to a height 1/14 of 34 feet. Having made this prediction, Torricelli performed a classical experiment to verify it.

The experiment, which must have been performed a countless number of times in school laboratories since Torricelli's time, is very simple to perform. Take a glass tube about 3 feet long, one end of which has a mouth about the width of the thumb, and fill it with mercury to the brim. Put the thumb over the mouth and upturn the tube, plunging the thumb end of it in a pan of mercury. Release the thumb making sure that the open end of the tube remains under the mercury in the pan. The top of the mercury column in the tube will drop slightly and oscillate for a while before coming to rest. The height of the mercury column from the surface of the mercury in the pan at this point is 2 and 3/7 feet (34/14 feet), as predicted.

Torricelli's experiment does not directly verify his notion about the atmosphere being a "sea of air," but, nevertheless, it gave tremendous support to the explanation of the behavior of the suction pump that the "sea of air" notion afforded. At any rate, this experiment was followed by a series that Blaise Pascal (1623–1662) carried out with the help of his brother-in-law, Perier. From Torricelli's explanation and experiment, Pascal deduced—predicted—that the mercury column supported by air pressure would be shorter on a high mountain. (The reader will recognize this as the principle behind the barometer.) This deduction was again aided by hydrostatics, of which Pascal was a master. Pascal knew that the pressure exerted by the weight of water is greater at the bottom and reasoned that if air is like water in this respect, the air pressure must be lower on the top of a mountain than at the bottom of it. Accordingly, he had his brother-in-law carry out the Torricelli experiment at various altitudes on Puy-de-Dôme, a mountain in Rouen, France. Perier observed that the mercury column was decidedly shorter at the summit than at the bottom, and that it had intermediate heights on the way up to the summit. It throws an interesting light on the nature of experiments of this kind to note that while Perier was scaling the mountain with the "barometer" he had a man stationed at the bottom of the mountain reading another "barometer." He also took several readings of the mercury column at the summit in varying conditions—under a shelter, in the open, under a passing cloud, etc. These precautions were taken to make sure that the variation in the mercury column observed on the mountain was not affected by other factors than the presumed air pressure. This experiment, incidentally, confirms the statement that air pressure varies inversely with altitude, which was introduced earlier in explaining the changes in the boiling point of water.

The theory of relativity furnishes a more spectacular example of how prediction relates to theory. From Newton's laws one could deduce that the light ray emanating from a star and passing in the vicinity of the sun would be bent by a certain small angle due to the gravitational force of the sun. According to Einstein's theory, however, this angle should be approximately double. The trouble with these deductions is that it is not often that a star lines up with the sun so that its light can be observed, and even when it does, it cannot be seen easily because of the brilliance of the sun. The confirmation of Einstein's theory thus had to await a total solar eclipse coinciding with the passing of a star at a critical angle. As luck would have it, there was to be such an event on May 29, 1919, just five years after Einstein formulated his new law of gravitation (general theory of relativity). So, in effect, a prediction was made that the ray from the star scheduled to pass by the sun on that day would be bent by an angle of a little less than 1¾ seconds. Needless to say, this prediction was borne out rather triumphantly by astronomical photographs taken on that day of solar eclipse. It might be added here that similar predictions were made for subsequent ecliptic occasions, all of which have been confirmed.

The confirmation of an explanation is not always attended by spectacular displays of this order, but dramatic demonstrations help establish the explanation psychologically.

2.

The process by which a prediction is derived from a theory is logically the same as the reconstructed structure of scientific explanation. In each case a statement is deduced from the theory; in the first case it refers to an event not yet observed, while in the second it is about a phenomenon already known. The word "prediction" is used here in a loose sense to refer to both the foretelling of things yet to happen and to the telling of events that have already taken place but not yet observed (by the explainer); the latter is sometimes called retrodiction (or postdiction). In this respect, prediction in science is like what a fortune teller does. A fortune teller looks not only into a man's future but also into his past and makes pronouncements about events he has not witnessed; either kinds of pronouncements are loosely referred to as fortune telling. In any event, the difference in the tense between pre- and retrodiction is not important from the point of view of understanding the significance of these activities in science. Both will therefore be referred to as prediction from now on.

Prediction serves the important function of testing the theory behind an explanation, and in this context it is often referred to as an hypothesis. A theory, whether it consists of a few generalizations of low-level abstraction or is constructed of diverse principles of high abstraction, as in physics, is always more general than the statements of the things or events to be explained; otherwise the latter could not be deduced from the theory, and there would be no explanation. By virtue of its generality, a theory implies more than what is being explained; that is, statements about other things or events can also be deduced from the same theory—these are what we mean by predictions, or hypotheses. Now, if the theory is correct, these other deductions must square with observable facts. This is the logic of testing a theory by prediction.

The reason why emphasis is placed on testing a theory by as yet unobserved events is to avoid a possible circularity. A theory is constructed to account for already known facts, and if all that can be deduced from the theory is one of these facts, the theory would be true by definition, and there would be no possibility of testing it. Such a theory may serve as a convenient summary of facts but could not advance our knowledge beyond what is already known. There are, of course, other tests of a theory, which have to do with the logical characteristics of the theory, such as inconsistency, circularity, and incompleteness of assumptions, characteristics that are often discernible in sociological explanations, as will be seen in Chapters VI, VII, and VIII. But these logical flaws can be looked at in the light of testing the consequences they entail. For instance, when a theory leads to consequences that are mutually contradictory, one of these has to be at odds with empirical observations, and the theory has to be placed under suspicion, even before the facts are ascertained.

If a prediction enabled by a theory, that is, an hypothesis, does not "pan out" upon investigation, the theory is discredited, or falsified. On the other hand, however, if a prediction is held up by facts, it does not prove the theory correct, but merely shows a lack of evidence that it is incorrect. In this court, as in the Anglo-Saxon legal system, a theory, as a defendant, is never given the verdict of "innocent," but only one of "guilty" or "not guilty." But the trial of a theory is never terminated, and the verdict of "not guilty," if such should be given, is only temporary until further evidence is uncovered to upset it. In this temporary state of grace, the theory is said to be verified, or confirmed. But such expressions, though used for convenience, should not give the impression that a confirmed theory is eternally true. The insecure state of scientific theories is doubtless responsible for the perennial changes, or as some would say the progress, in science, and drives scientists to their continuous activity of testing and refining theories.

The reason why a theory can be given only a temporary bill of clearance can be seen by considering a simple example constructed by Bertrand Russell. If a theory posits, one, that bread is made of stones and, two, that stones are nourishing, it follows that bread is nourishing. And as long as bread can be shown to be nourishing, this theory is verified, according to the rule of science. In this instance, of course, the premises that bread is made of stones and that stones are nourishing are empirical statements that can be directly checked against facts, and for this reason we know this theory to be false. But suppose that a theory contains premises that are not empirical in this sense and that only their consequences (predictions) can be empirically tested, as is usually the case with most theories. Then we would have no choice but to accept the theory as confirmed, or not falsified, upon verifying the deductions. If we feel uncomfortable about accepting this verdict, for whatever reason, we will have to keep on searching for the evidence that will falsify it.

Logically speaking, one only needs a single contrary instance to falsify a universal statement, and it might be thought that it is a clear-cut matter to put a theory out of business with a crucial experiment or observation. But empirical testing in science, in the final analysis, is not a question of logic but of perception, admitting of uncertainties and gradations, for observation is not possible without human perception, and the latter is fallible. The judgment of whether or not a prediction is fulfilled, therefore, cannot be made categorically but only in degrees, and at what point we declare a prediction confirmed is more or less indeterminate. In Torricelli's experiment, for instance, the height of the mercury column will not always register exactly 2 and 3/7 feet; in a particular trial it might be 2 and ½ feet. Such discrepancies result from variations in the laboratory conditions that are not fully controlled, such as temperature, atmospheric pressure, purity of mercury, etc., and from the fluctuation in the observer's perception. Under the circumstances, whether or not the reading of the mercury column at 2 and ½ feet, instead of the theoretical value, confirms the theory is decided, not by logic, but by the prevailing standards among practicing scientists. Furthermore, the abstract nature of the theory usually leaves room for "interpreting" the correspondence between theoretical terms and the terms employed in empirical predictions, and this circumstance more or less shields the theory from being tarnished by the fate of the predictions.

Especially in sociology, concepts, such as social disintegration, are abstract and their concrete referents are not clearly determinable. If, for instance, a high divorce rate in a society indicates a state of social disintegration, as often assumed, does the breaking up of extended families also signify the same thing? These characteristics prevail even in sophisticated sciences such as physics, though, to be sure, not to the same crippling extent as in sociology. Granted, then, that it is impossible to prove a theory true, it is not so easy to disprove it either. At any rate, it is not as easy as disproving a false theorem in geometry, which does not require empirical tests. It is for this reason that "bad" theories persist, sometimes even in the face of uncomfortable facts. The phlogiston theory held out for a hundred or so years, because it was full of escape hatches that made it difficult for it to come to grips with empirical data. And many a sociological theory persists today for the same reason.

3.

The deductions that have been considered so far, whether used for explanation or prediction, are based on generalizations that are universal statements. A universal statement is one which asserts that in all cases satisfying certain conditions a specified event will occur; for example, whenever the altitude increases, the atmospheric pressure drops. It is, however, possible to explain and make predictions on the basis of general statements that are not universal but statistical. A statistical statement gives the probability with which a specified event will occur among the cases of certain characteristics; for example, the probability that a twenty-one-year-old will survive in a given year is .9921 (about 99 in 100). From such a statement it cannot be deduced that an instance of the event in question will occur, namely, that a particular twenty-one-year-old will live. Hence, it cannot be used to explain deductively why a particular youth aged twenty-one lives through the year. But it gives the probability that he will live, which in this instance is rather high, and in this, perhaps inductive, sense, the statistical statement in conjunction with others might be said to explain the occurrence of the event in a particular case.

It is possible to derive, by the probability calculus, the probability of an event from several generalizations of a statistical nature impinging on it, and hence to make predictions as well as explanations of a statistical nature. And there are determinate interpretations of probability statements to make the predictions testable. That is, a statistical statement is not to be confused with a vague one, as it often tends to be. For instance, a statement that the probability that a twenty-one-year-old will live is .9921 is to be contrasted with a statement such as that the survival rate among twenty-one-year-olds is high. The first statement can be compared with actual death statistics to see if, in fact, 9,921 out of 10,000 twenty-one-year-olds manage to live through a given year, and if, where there is a descrepancy, it is small enough to be reasonably attributed to chance fluctuations in the samples of twenty-one-year-olds observed. In this process, the decision to accept or not to accept an observational discrepancy of a given size as negligible is typically accompanied by a numerical indication of how large a risk is involved of being wrong. Consequently, depending on how much of a gambler one is, one can be satisfied with more or less rough correspondence between the predicted and actual outcomes, although in practice the size of risk tends to be fixed within certain limits by a convention among practicing scientists. In this respect, there are elements of indeterminacy and arbitrariness in testing a statistical statement. These elements are, of course, also present in the second statement merely asserting that the survival of the age group in question is high. But clearly the range of values that can satisfy this vague statement is indeterminately large and the decision to accept an actual survival rate as confirming this statement is not guided by any objective standard that can be inspected by others.

In a sense, all predictive statements in science may be thought of as being statistically interpreted in the context of verification. For instance, in the Torricelli experiment, the prediction that the mercury will rise 2 and 3/7 feet in the upturned tube is checked typically against several readings of the mercury column, which give a kind of statistical basis for evaluating the efficacy of the prediction, whether or not a formal statistical analysis is carried out. From this point of view, all sciences, including classical physics, may be considered statistical. But more commonly a theory in which the basic principles are stated in probability terms and in which calculus of probability is used in the process of deducing explanations and predictions is referred to as a statistical theory. What makes a theory statistical is thus not in the verificational end of it but in the very beginning where the basic premises are set forth.

The resulting difference between a strictly deductive explanation and one that is based on statistical generalizations, which cannot be discussed in this space, may be important from a logical point of view, but for the present purpose both types of explanation can be treated together, since in each case the explanation (and prediction) follows from generalizations (scientific laws), whether these are universal or statistical. I will, therefore, use "deduction," somewhat loosely, to mean the process of deriving a specific statement, whether categorical or probabilistic, from general statements (scientific laws), whether universal or statistical. It is important to note this terminological slur here, since empirical generalizations, and theories, in sociology are likely to be statistical in nature, and in this sense the strictly deductive model of explanation in classical physics might be said to be inappropriate if emphasis is placed on the logical aspect of the deductive procedure. In any event, a sociological explanation is not necessarily rendered more difficult to be tested just because it is to be statistically constructed and hence is not exempt from the usual empirical requirements for verification.

In the way of a summary, the significance of prediction in science is not in the glamour of prophecy but in the empirical verification of an explanation that it makes possible. The process of verifying an explanation in science involves deductive reasoning, as in proving a logical truth in, say, geometry. The former, however, is contingent upon relevant observations, a circumstance that gives a temporary character to a scientific explanation: it is valid only as long as it "works." Modern scientific theories tend to be statistical in that the general principles leading to explanation and prediction are probability statements, the process of deriving explanatory and predictive statements involves the calculus of probability, and observational data are assessed by statistical criteria. The use of statistics in modern science objectifies the handling of uncertainties and fluctuations in observational data, and thus *reduces* the subjective element in the verificational phase of science. In any event, it does not change the hierarchical and logical aspects of science in which a prediction, or an hypothesis, is derived from general principles by explicit rules of reasoning. Statistics in sociology as in other sciences, therefore, does not diminish the need for an explanation that can stand up to empirical tests.

IV. Technology:
The Question of Utility

THE JUSTIFICATION of sociology in the minds of many who profess it, as well as those who finance sociological research, rests on its promise of utility. Sociology, on the one hand, is thought to be worthy of support because it would help solve social problems and make the world a "better" place to live in, and grappling with social problems, on the other, is said to help sociology develop as a science, a "pure" science. Undoubtedly there is an element of truth in this apologia of current sociological practices. But a social problem-oriented sociology betrays our deep-seated tendency to view the world as evolving around us, for our benefit, and to construct conceptual schemes premised on the criteria of "good" and "bad," "right" and "wrong"— that is, to view a phenomenon as conforming to or deviating from our norm. The use of more antiseptic sounding words, such as "eufunction" vs. "dysfunction," "integration" vs. "disintegration," "stability" vs. "instability," not to speak of more charged words, such as "abnormal behavior," "social deviation," only thinly disguises the basic self-centered cosmology of modern sociology. There is, of course, no intrinsic reason why the world should not be thought of as evolving around us, but that this orientation does not necessarily produce the most effective explanation in scientific terms is well attested to by the development of modern science following the Copernican revolution which broke the spell holding captive man's mind in an earthbound image of the universe. The center of the universe for modern sociology is, of course, not the earth; nor is it so much *homo sapiens,* nor the Victorian gentleman. These have

44

been demoted from the exalted position by the ripples emanating from the Copernican quake. It is rather the twentieth-century bourgeois, and it is his ideals in terms of which social phenomena are viewed, some as normative, some as problems.

Sociology, of course, should not be insensitive to man's problems, and if it can solve some of these problems, so much the better. But science as a viable intellectual activity is not necessarily promoted by exclusive preoccupation with practical problems, and in a sense, the instrumental benefits of science, its technological applications, are due to its very penchant to supersede and ignore practical ends. An appreciation of this somewhat subtle relationship between the epistemic and practical aspects of science is an essential step toward removing the constrictive mold of a self-centered world view clamped on modern sociology.

How are practical consequences derived from science? The link between a scientific theory and its practical application is deduction, the structure of which is the same as in deriving a prediction, an hypothesis, to test. Not all deductions from an explanation serve the purpose of testing the explanation, although every consequence of an explanation, every prediction made possible by the explanation, carries with it a seed of verification. The deduction that water boils at a higher temperature in a pressure cooker than in an ordinary pan is no longer an hypothesis to be tested but a principle derived from a well-tested theory that is put to work in aid of housewives. The phenomenon of heat absorption accompanying evaporation, another principle derivable from the same theory, is used in manufacturing refrigerators. Or, the prediction that there will be a lunar eclipse on January 30, 1972, is no more to be doubted than the trivial one that the sun will rise tomorrow; if we think about this prediction at all, we might note the date on our calendars to remind us to observe the spectacle of the moon being swallowed up in the shadow of the earth. The most awesome display of the power of scientific prediction is furnished by the atom bomb, the basic principle of which derives from Einstein's special theory of relativity. By the time the United States government made the decision to manufacture the bomb, there was no doubt in the minds of scientists that it could be done on the basis of the demonstrated soundness of the theory. The prediction pointing to the atom bomb had only to be implemented politically and technologically.

Much of modern technology clearly derives from the explanatory power of science, and the success of technology bestows prestige upon science. In the mind of the general public this relationship is sometimes exaggerated, and science is equated with technology. That is, technology is thought to be possible only because of science, and science is considered wonderful because it produces useful technology. This view, however, overstates the relationship between science and technology.

First of all, technical tools and skills, whether or not these are dignified by the term "technology," are often acquired before and independently of science. Consider the first wheel invented by man. It probably resulted from a process combining a measure of accident, a measure of trial and error, and a measure of reasoning, but without being accompanied—and certainly without being preceded—by an explanation as to why it works. The first man-made fire was most likely to have been even more of a product of accident and less of reasoning, not to speak of explanation. To cite a couple of historically documented cases, the ancient Egyptians had the know-how to construct pyramids without the benefit of Newtonian mechanics (or any kind of mechanics, for that matter), and tinkers from antiquity to the beginning of the nineteenth century knew how to win metals from ores and to forge alloys of metals without being able to explain the processes involved. A form of the steam engine, which heralded the British industrial revolution, was invented around the beginning of the eighteenth century by an artisan, a "mechanic," who could not and did not know the thermodynamics involved. How could he have, considering the fact that in those days combustion was explained rather quaintly by a hazy concept called phlogiston, and water was still thought to be one of the four basic elements, the others being air, fire, and earth? James Watt, the name most often associated with the steam engine, introduced a much improved model about half a century later, but he was an instrument maker, an "engineer" in modern terminology, who obviously did not have the theoretical explanation of how steam does the work—an explanation that does not come until later in the history of science.

Second, it is not only through scientific explanations that useful predictions are made. The ancient Babylonians could predict lunar eclipses from a long series of observations. (At the time of Alexander the Great, the Babylonians are said to have accumulated records of lunar eclipses extending over 1,900 years.) But they could not *explain* this familiar phenomenon, in the sense of deducing it from more general principles, nor seemingly were they interested in doing so. To jump to predictions of different kinds and of recent times, life insurance companies have been making predictions, at least for the last two centuries, about life expectancies of different age groups with enough accuracy to make the venture enormously profitable. These predictions are projections based on average rates of death calculated over a period of time. They make the simple assumptions that the aggregate conditions producing the current rates will prevail in the future, and that, if they change, the change itself will follow the trend of the past. Here there is no attempt to account for the conditions producing the rates, the persistence of the conditions, or if the conditions change, for the direction of the change. More recently, during the past few presidential elections, public opinion pollsters have made close enough predictions of electoral results to make their activities a going concern as a marketable service to politicians. But these electoral predictions are mere indications of how prospective voters will vote within a short period of time, based on verbal reports of a representative sample; the accuracy of the predictions drops off to a useless level beyond a few months. In comparison with the success of the pollsters, the current political theories are woefully inadequate as explanations of voting behavior, as is apparent from their inability to make reliable, long-range predictions of voting.

There is a widely held view that science is born of the necessity to solve practical problems. The example often cited in support of this contention is that of geometry, allegedly growing out of the ancient Egyptians' need to build pyramids for the kings and to survey land to collect taxes from the people. But Egyptian geometry remained a practical art of surveying and drafting without reaching the level of abstract codification; the workings of geometry were not explained by way of deductive proof from general principles. This failure becomes obvious when considered in the light of Greek geometry, which Herodotus said originated in Egypt. Geometry is an abstract axiomatic system of knowledge developed in the hands of ancient Greeks, as every schoolboy knows. It was the Greeks' love of learning as opposed to the Egyptians' love of riches, as Plato put it, which made this development possible. And similarly it was the Greeks' drive to explain the phenomena of the senses in terms of general principles that is responsible for their achievement in incipient sciences as well as in mathematics and philosophy.

During the period roughly corresponding to the golden age of Greek learning, China had the most developed technical skills of all the world, obviously catering to various needs of a civilized society, and made important beginnings in scientific endeavors, including mathematics. But somehow Chinese science never caught up with its technology, which again suggests that technology and science are propelled by different forces.

The more recent history of science fails also to show modern science springing up to meet technological demands. Modern science has its origins in philosophy, a generalized body of knowledge, and it was called natural philosophy even in the days of Newton. To be sure, science has had a symbiotic relationship with technology, but the direction of benefit has not always been from science to technology. For at least two centuries, from the seventeenth on, it was more from technology to science. The invention of measuring instruments, such as the telescope, microscope (both probably accidental inventions by lens makers), air pump, barometer, and thermometer, may not have heralded the Scientific Revolution but undoubtedly spurred it on once it was set in motion. Also, the practical knowledge of the artisans during the early stages of modern science exercised scientists' intellectual curiosity. The metallurgists of the eighteenth century knew how to calcify metal and to obtain vitriolic (sulfuric) acid from sulfur, and artisans of the same century could make steam to turn an engine. But it was the impractical men of learning in the pay of princes or universities, mulling over the principles behind these phenomena in search of explanations, who prepared the way for the discovery of gases and understanding heat as a form of energy. Kepler, the man who completed the Copernican revolution in astronomy, is supposed to have been motivated to study astronomy by his desire to show the course of the divine work. This motivation, which may seem rather unscientific in the present-day context, was not atypical of sixteenth- and seventeenth-century scientists; it is compatible with the search for explanation and is closer to it in spirit than approaching science for the practical results it can produce. The contribution of science to technology was not spectacular until about a hundred years ago, and the scientist during the incubating period of modern science was apparently help up to ridicule for wasting time with useless activities—much as modern professors, including sociologists, occasionally are by the would-be men of practical wisdom.

It is not an easy matter to decide to what extent the development of science was fostered by its potential utility. Undoubtedly, the Renaissance princes who patronized scientists were at least partially motivated by the prospect of practical advantages that they might gain from the employment of scientists, as well as by their love of pure learning. And for men like Galileo, who was immersed in technical projects of various kinds, technological problems must have been a constant source of challenge to explanation and experimentation. In recent times, science as a whole is said to have been subjected to the same sort of influence exerted by modern technological industries.

Thus science has drawn on practical arts in its growth, and it has been stimulated by practical needs, however indirectly. But in its basic aims and activities, it is fundamentally removed from practical solutions of immediate problems. It is not concerned with just making a suction pump work better or making more powerful steam engines, but with explaining how a suction pump works or how and why steam does the work it does. In this quest for explanation the scientist poses more and more general questions transcending the practical problem. And, paradoxically, the scientist's contribution to the solution of practical problems lies in his ability and inclination to bypass and leave behind the concrete, the immediate. Without the explanatory feature of science, not only would we be deprived of the intrinsic intellectual satisfaction afforded by it, but also our technology would be a mere shadow of what it is. Alchemy, which sought to reap a rich harvest by converting common metals to gold, was singularly devoid of the spirit of quest for explanation, and was even sterile of useful results. The whole adventure finally collapsed without having contributed much to the chemical riches to follow with the advent of modern science. In this perspective, the benefit accruing from the recent massive technological demands made on science could be exaggerated and their long-range effects, which may not be all positive, remain to be evaluated by the future historians of science.

It seems, then, that the relationship between science and utility is not a simple one. On the one hand, the Greek love of speculation and abstraction stopped short of producing mature empirical sciences. Having made ingenious beginnings in conceptual schemes, the Greeks apparently lacked interest in practical knowledge. On the other hand, however, many useful technological inventions that sprang up in different civilizations, ancient and not so ancient, were produced without the benefit of scientific understanding and were not followed by the devel-

opment of science as we know it today. It is, of course, a moot
question, if it is a meaningful one to ask at all, whether individual scientists are motivated by the practical results that science
is capable of yielding. Evidence suggests that most scientists'
motivation is somewhat more ethereal than this.

If sociology is today not an enviable science, it is not for the
lack of technical skills, intellectual curiosity, or practical
purpose. There is actually a tradition of practical work in sociology which has produced techniques of social investigation, if not
of effective social engineering. One strand of this tradition stems
from the welfare-minded inquiries, mainly of nineteenth-century
England, which has led to the development of survey techniques
widely used in sociology today. The other goes back to the practice of collecting civic statistics, which occupied some men of
learning in seventeenth- and eighteenth-century Europe and has
contributed to the discipline of statistics permeating aspects of
modern sociology. The speculative bent in sociological thinking
is, of course, as old as man, the more explicit and systematic
conceptual schemes having been developed, mostly in Europe,
and handed down to us over the last fifty years or more. Thus
modern sociology has not been entirely lacking in the tools for
answering the more practical problems, no more than in speculative thinking. The need for making sociology a socially useful
activity has also been keenly felt. Despite all this, however, sociology remains an ineffective science, and the reason, I suggest,
lies in the particular conceptual orientation which has
prevented the joint germination of explanation, verification, and
application.

Science may not exist by or for technology, but the fact remains that science leads to practical applications of immense
utility, the kind not possible without its benefit. And its achievement is made possible by the logical structure of verification by
prediction, which is in turn the same as the logical structure of
explanation by deduction. All these flow from the same source,
the theory, by the same deductive process, and terminate in
tangible results. Thus, where there is a valid explanation, there

is satisfactory verification, and where this obtains, there is successful application; and vice versa. Explanation, verification, and
application all hang together and rest on the same empirical
foundation. Herein lies the power, as well as the charm, of science, which appeals to both the pragmatic and the speculative.
But this union is wrought at the cost of imposing a constraint on
what we mean by explanation and thereby restricting the range
of speculation, for a theory that cannot participate in this trian-
gle of empirical relevance cannot function as a scientific explanation. A theory, in particular, which is formulated in the
framework of what is normative or "natural" appeals to what is
intuitively "self-evident," to anticipate the discussion to follow
in the next chapter, and hence preempts the empirical enterprise of validation and of application. And this is the clue to the
paradox that *a sociology preoccupied with practical problems is
in the end self-defeating.*

V. The Scientific Revolution: Common Sense, Aristotle, Galileo

I T IS an often repeated allegation that sociology is mere common sense. This is of course an unfair slander if it means that sociologists do not command facts and techniques of data manipulation that are not readily available to the man in the street. But in a more fundamental sense sociology is bound up with common sense in a much tighter grip than might appear from a cursory look at sociological outpourings. The key concepts lying at the bottom of current sociological explanations are notions running through homely wisdom, and the basic scheme of sociological explanation itself bears the image of what passes for an explanation in everyday discourse. Both the content and the style of common sense explanation stand in the way of a scientifically viable explanation. The Aristotelian cosmology, which was, in essence, systematized common sense, arrested the development of medieval physics as a science, and it was with the breaking of this conceptual mold that modern science was born. This is the lesson to be drawn from the Scientific Revolution for the sociology of tomorrow.

1.

The common sense explanation, say, of suicide, might be rendered without adornment: "Unhappiness causes suicide." It is this simple-minded formula that is turned around to show how unhappy, for instance, Marilyn Monroe was, or how miserable the Swedes or the American Indians are. To be sure, unhappiness is often further attributed to other causal factors: Hollywood

drove Marilyn Monroe to loneliness; the welfare state robs a
person of purpose in life; the life on reservations gives young
Indians no hope of a future—such loneliness, lack of purpose, and
hopelessness being understood to entail unhappiness. But whatever the circumstances leading to unhappiness, the fatal connection between this condition and suicide is accepted as common
sense. Why?

The statement that unhappiness causes suicide is compelling
because its converse, "a suicide is unhappy," is essentially a
definition of unhappiness, to the extent that the man in the
street, the guardian of common sense, is not given to identifying
unhappy men independently of the act of suicide and then ascertaining that unhappy men are inclined to suicide. That is, as
long as we tend to conclude, subsequent to the act of suicide
and on the strength of it alone, that the suicide was an unhappy
man, the statement linking unhappiness to suicide merely
specifies a class of people to be considered unhappy. When a
definition is used as an explanatory proposition, this is of course
true by the terms of the definition, and the explanation is a
circularity. When we see a dog eating the food set in front of
him at a furious speed, we "explain" that he eats that way because he is very hungry. But since in all likelihood we come to
equate a dog's hunger with the way he eats, this "explanation"
merely asserts that the dog is eating avidly, a circularity.

The tautology involved in this kind of common sense explanation is often not so blatantly obvious because the definition involved is usually not explicitly stated in precisely the terms
constituting the would-be explanation. For example, we also refer
to people as unhappy even though they are not suicides, and we
recognize a hungry dog not by his manner of eating alone. But
to the extent that the state of unhappiness is not explicitly
defined in terms specifically excluding the act of suicide, the
element of circularity is not avoided in the unhappiness explanation of suicide. The vague feeling that unhappiness can be
defined independently of suicide only camouflages the logical
pitfall involved.

One factor contributing to the pervasiveness of concepts like "unhappiness" that figure in common sense explanation is that they refer to introspective states we can recognize as part of our own experience. We "know," for instance, what it is like to be unhappy, and we can "imagine" the acuteness of this feeling reaching the point where life is no longer supportable and is terminated. Similarly, most of us have had the experience of being hungry and, upon finding food, devouring it with great gusto. But the fact that we have all experienced what we refer to as "unhappiness" or "hunger" does not mean that we can objectively identify an unhappy man or a hungry dog with a degree of agreement among ourselves, a step that must be taken in order to substantiate explanations in scientific terms. Of course, not every statement in an explanation has to be empirically verified, as was pointed out in Chapter II, so that concepts such as "unhappiness" or "hunger," it might be argued, do not have to be given direct empirical interpretations; they might be thought analogous to theoretical terms in science. But typically a common sense explanation furnishes no guide to how statements underlying such would-be theoretical terms might lead to statements of empirical relevance. A term such as "unhappiness," which is in the vocabulary of every man, conceals the fact that it carries a different set of personal experiences for each, and as long as the individual experience is relied upon as the criterion of an unhappy man, such a term cannot be given an objective meaning. The trouble with introspectively familiar concepts in common sense explanations is not so much that they refer to subjective and therefore not directly observable entities; after all, the referents of theoretical concepts in science, such as "molecules," "gravity," and "genes," are unobservable. It is rather that their familiarity deceives us into thinking that the explanatory propositions featuring them have empirical and objective validity, when in reality they only give us tautologies, propositions that are true by definition.

Explanations involving "need," "want," "desire," and "liking" are as prevalent in common sense as the ones premised on

"unhappiness" (or "happiness") and run the same risk of producing circular arguments. "Explaining" a man's excessive smoking
by saying that he likes to smoke is an obvious example.
(Nowadays we are likely to explain instead that the excessive
smoker is "orally fixated," but as long as the state of oral
fixation is not identified independently of the smoking behavior,
the logical problem involved is the same; "oral fixation" is but a
fancy cover for a simple tautological idea.) A child who, upon
being asked why he twists his hair, answers "because I want to"
gives a tautological explanation in its most unadulterated form.
We recognize this, with exasperation, as a pseudo-explanation,
because the child is clearly being circular; he is only telling us
what he wants to do at that moment. Explanations making use
of these concepts may appear to be overly trite exhibits of
common sense reasoning when expressed in such simple sentences as "Unhappiness causes suicide" or "A man smokes a lot
because he likes it." But a moment's reflection will show that
they are ingrained in our daily thinking with or without much
disguise.

These familiar concepts are also at the roots of sociological
explanations, although the use of elaborate data, strange terminology, obtuse language, and technical expertise tend to obscure
this fact. It is true that at the level where working sociologists
are engaged in collecting and analyzing data to show empirical
relationships between relevant factors, say, suicide rate and religious affiliation, there is little that resembles common sense
practices. But in the context of explanation where these empirical relationships enter as supporting evidence, the common
sense conceptual habit manifests itself. Durkheim, for example,
made extensive and imaginative use of suicide statistics to show
the relationship between suicide rate and religious affiliation,
marital status, occupational position, and economic conditions,
with which he sought to establish the effect of social disintegration on suicide. But he went on to explain this relationship,
which, incidentally, he insisted was a social fact. He ended up
by unabashedly resorting to "unhappiness," "despair," "will to

live," and other intuitively appealing terms that refer to feelings
of the individual. These homely touches, however, did not add
scientific validity to Durkheim's explanation of suicide, which
was meticulously built up on ingenious analysis of extensive
data.

Lurking behind every common sense explanation relying on
"desire," "need," and the like, there is the notion of "purpose,"
and when such an explanation is pushed for further elucidation,
a reference to a purpose or a goal is not too long in coming to
provide the clinching argument. For example, a typical chain of
argument might be telescoped as follows: "A mother loves her
child because she needs to love, so the child may be nurtured
and, ultimately, so the human race may be preserved." The
teleological idea that human behavior is purposive, or as sociologists would say goal-oriented, is implicit in common sense
thinking and asserts itself with the force of a self-evident truth.
The overriding purpose of human behavior, the ultimate in the
train of purposes, and of needs, wants, etc., as well, is commonly thought to be the pursuit of pleasure, or, at any rate, the
avoidance of pain. This belief, often referred to as the pleasure
principle, has been with us a long time and is not easy to
shake off. It would appear inconceivable in the common sense
order of things that human behavior can be viewed in some other
way, without reference to "purpose," that the goal-oriented conception is just one of possible outlooks on nature. Human behavior "*is*," we say, *not* "can be viewed as," purposive. It is a
well-entrenched thought-habit not easily dislodged.

One does not have to dig very deeply into the foundation of
modern sociology to encounter this conceptual matrix of common sense. It is evident, and sometimes even explicit, in the
dominant school of current sociology, which Talcott Parsons has
called the "voluntaristic" tradition, of which Parsons himself is a
leading exponent, and it is expressed indirectly through the
functionalist approach, which evolves around the notion of
"functional needs." These two currents are of course often
confluent, as in Parsons' sociology, and between the two they

account for nearly all that goes on in the way of explaining in sociology. Even in the remaining small area, overtones of teleology, if not direct references of "purpose," are frequent enough to reinforce the common sense heritage of sociology. But more about this later, in the next three chapters.

Common sense, in applying teleological explanations, does not stop with human behavior, social or individual. We hear people say, for example, "It rains so things can grow," or "We have lungs so we can breathe," as if they were giving reasons why we use fertilizers or hearing-aids. Such extensions of teleology to natural phenomena, to the point of postulating, however implicitly, human-like agents (which make things grow or enable people to breathe), let the cat out of the common sense bag.

Explanations that refer to "desire," "want," "need," etc., no less than those relating to "purpose," treat the phenomena being explained, whether or not human, as if they were produced by agents who have, and can on request give, reasons for their actions, much as a man can tell us why he carries an umbrella in the rain or takes aspirin. Reason giving is a very prevalent way of answering "why" questions in everyday practice, and the reasons most frequently given have to do with our purpose, desire, need, want, etc. But not every "why-because" exchange eliciting this kind of reason constitutes a scientific explanation. Often a "why" question is an invitation to a conversation, as in the succession of whys that children barrage adults with; or it may carry a rebuke, as when an adult asks a child why he spilled the milk. "Because" answers, correspondingly, may only furnish chit-chat or convenient excuses, neither of which necessarily exclude circularity and other logically flawed arguments as valid modes of communication. Some "why" questions, of course, demand explanations, to which it would be irrelevant to give "because" answers of communicative nature. Common sense explanations are often this kind of inappropriate "because" answers given to "why" questions calling for explanations. Consequently, would-be scientific explanations predicated on reasons featured in "because" answers of common sense cannot, with ease, if at all, extricate themselves from the morass of a-logicality inherent in human communication.

Common sense, including introspective explanatory concepts, especially "purpose," was codified and built into the Aristotelian cosmology. Medieval physics, which was based on this philosophy, visualized a universe in which things happened with purpose and by preordained rules. It was a system which could give "because" answers to all "why" questions, but one which could not give explanations that could be tested empirically or that could lead to practical consequences. It was by overthrowing this system that modern science was made possible.

2.

Science is often thought to *grow out of* common sense. In one sense of the word, science is indeed based on common sense. This is the sense that refers to the commonality of human perception and reasoning. This aspect of common sense might be called common sensibility in distinction to the other aspect, which might be called common conception, embracing generally available factual knowledge. Now, the business of science is very much dependent on common sensibility, for without agreement in our sense judgment the basic measurements of science are not possible, and without sharing rules of reasoning science would cease to be the public activity that it is. But where common conception is concerned, it is rather understating the case to say that science grows out of it in the sense of gradual refinement and sophistication. To be sure, in the initial stages of a science the explanations advanced are characterized by the use of implicit assumptions and intuitively meaningful concepts. But the manner in which common sense is replaced by science is more a revolution than an evolution. It is not merely that assumptions get stated more explicitly, and deductions made more formally; nor merely that terms get more precisely defined and quantified and that measurement becomes more sophisticated with the aid of improved instruments. All these things assuredly happen in the course of scientific development. But the really crucial change is in the revamping of the common sense conceptual mold, and this change is not a matter of degree, but is radical and discrete. Moving the center of the universe from the earth to the sun was upsetting to the cosmological view of the middle ages, but the conceptual change that was brought about by the time Galileo died and Newton was born, a change largely due to Galileo himself, was more drastic and more fundamental than the so-called Copernican revolution for the development of the modern science.

This change can be appreciated by comparing the medieval view of mechanics with its transformation brought about by Galileo. In the Middle Ages all motion was thought to require a mover. This is a common sense generalization of what we observe. Nothing moves unless it is pushed, pulled, or carried by some agent. According to the Aristotelian cosmology of the Middle Ages, the center of the universe is the spherical earth, which is engulfed in layers of water, air, and fire. Surrounding these spherical envelopes are crystalline spheres in each of which is embedded a "planet," i.e., the moon, Mercury, Venus, the sun, Mars, Jupiter, and Saturn. These concentric spheres, which wrap each other like layers of an onion, are in turn enveloped by an overall crystalline sphere studded with the fixed stars. This universe is divided into two regions: one terrestrial, composed of the earth, water, air, and fire, and the other celestial, embracing the remaining spheres, from the moon on out. The celestial spheres, together with the planets stuck in them, are set in motion and kept in a state of mobility by the sphere of the fixed stars, which itself moves. This is the prime mover. Now, the natural motion of the celestial bodies is a circular one, this being the most perfect kind attainable by physical bodies. The movement of this prime mover was explained by saying, vaguely, that it aspires to attain the state of God, which is eternal rest, but, being only physical, the closest it can approach this state is an eternal circular motion. In other words, the purpose of the celestial activity is to be God-like, and its natural form is a circular motion.

In the terrestrial region, the Aristotelian view held, motion is caused by bodies seeking their natural place, and the natural form of the terrestrial motion is a straight line. A stone falls to the ground because the earth is its home. For similar reasons, air rises above water, and fire shoots up in the air. The Aristotelians maintained that the velocity of a moving body is proportional to the motive force. Thus, a heavier body falls faster than a lighter one, because the former has more of the matter that desires to be united with its own element. A falling body also gains speed as it approaches the ground because, as it gets closer to home, the more joyously it heads for it. With falling bodies, their gravity, as opposed to their levity, is the natural cause of motion. A terrestrial body would remain eternally at rest except for "violence," which causes it to move horizontally or "unnaturally," as when it is removed from its natural place of rest. Thus, the Aristotelian physics of the Middle Ages was normative and saw purpose in motion (which was called the final cause), in conformity with Aristotelian philosophy, which defined the nature of things and explained their behavior in terms of the goals to which they are directed. In this respect the lineage of modern sociology, which construes man's behavior as goal-directed and as conforming to or deviating from norms, goes back to the Aristotelian cosmology, which is in turn rooted in common sense.

Three centuries after the heyday of Aristotelian physics, when Galileo came to the problem of explaining the movement of bodies, he discarded the distinction between the celestial and the terrestrial. As a matter of fact, his works in mechanics were to serve as powerful arguments in establishing the Copernican thesis of a heliocentric universe. He then ignored gravity as a cause of motion, not being interested in what causes motion, or the agent, but rather in the observable regularities that could be generalized into mathematical relations. I quote Galileo himself through his spokesman, Salviati, from his *Dialogue Concerning the Two Chief World Systems;* Simplicio, the straight man, speaks first:

SIMP. The cause of this effect [of earthly things falling downward] is well known; everybody is aware that it is gravity.

SALV. You are wrong, Simplicio; what you ought to say is that everyone knows that it is called "gravity." What I am asking you for is not the name of the thing, but its essence, of which essence you know not a bit more than you know about the essence of whatever moves the stars around. I except (sic.) the name which has been attached to it and which has been made a familiar household word by the continual experience that we have of it daily. But we do not really understand what principle or what force it is that moves stones downward, any more than we understand what moves them upward after they leave the thrower's hand, or what moves the moon around. We have merely, as I said, assigned to the first the more specific and definite name "gravity," whereas to the second we assign the more general term "impressed force" . . . , and to the last named we give "spirits" . . . , either "assisting" . . . or "abiding" . . . ; and as the cause of infinite other motions we give "Nature."

Galileo thus set out not to explain why things move to begin with, but to describe in a generalized way how things move. In so doing, he abandoned the notions of "naturalness" and "purpose" in motion. Herein lies the revolution in the scientific outlook. It is not that Galileo refined or otherwise improved upon the causal explanations of Aristotelian mechanics, but rather that he postponed and actually banished the questions concerning the causes of motion. Consequently Galileo proceeded to study how bodies in motion behave and to formulate simple mathematical laws governing this behavior with the premise that motion is a state of nature requiring no explanation, which eliminated the prime mover with its human-like qualities from the explanatory scheme. He postulated that a body in motion continues moving in a straight line, without being moved continually by a mover, until it is opposed or altered by some force. This assumption, this way of looking at things, is startlingly at odds with the comfortably common sense view that things are moved by agents.

3.

Galileo felt that mathematical relations explain physical phenomena as long as the deductions obtained from them are in agreement with observable events. This is in contrast to the Aristotelian view that mathematics is insufficient for causal explanation of physical things, though useful for formal descriptions. In this, Galileo was indebted to the Platonism and Pythagoreanism of the Middle Ages, which regarded mathematical concepts as realities of ideal form. The elevation of mathematically expressible relationships to the status of enduring principles that explain observable phenomena had two related consequences for the conduct of science. First, the mathematical principles, or laws, were to be arrived at by making observations on selected aspects of a body in motion and correlations were to be made among them by means of mathematical relations. Accordingly, Galileo was to concentrate on the aspects of moving bodies that could be measured and rendered mathematically, ignoring those that could not be so treated. Second, abstract mathematical formulations led to experiments that could not have been suggested by physical causes of the common sense variety. For example, in his famous study of falling bodies, he singled out the distance and the time traveled by a moving body, both measurable attributes, and tried to analyze the relationship between them by rolling polished balls on an inclined plane. He resorted to this mechanical device because freely falling bodies travel too fast to be measured adequately by the techniques available at the time. He was convinced, rightly, that the general effect of acceleration is the same on an inclined plane as in a free fall, except that it is retarded in the first case according to the degree of inclination. Upon some preliminary trials, he formulated the hypothesis that the distance traversed by a moving body is proportional to the time traveled, and established it as a law by confirming it with experimental data. In setting up this hypothesis he assumed that the velocity of a falling body is incremented at a constant rate, that is, the acceleration is constant.

This assumption, it must be pointed out, was arrived at after false starts, one of which was that the increase in the velocity is proportional to the distance traveled. This was discarded because a mathematical consequence of this assumption is that it would take an infinite time to start a motion, a physical impossibility.

Measurement in experimental settings played an important role in establishing mathematical principles of motion, but it would be erroneous to think that this development was brought about by advancement in sophisticated instruments. The conceptual revolution under consideration took place before the invention of the telescope, microscope, theremometer, and precise clocks. As a matter of fact, Galileo used the flow of water from a large container with a hole in it to measure time intervals, and the experimental results he obtained were very rough by our standards. Nevertheless, Galileo's conceptualization developed along the lines of available, and often crude, measurements (e.g., time and distance) that were short extensions of everyday practices. It is from this empirical source of common usage, rather than from any fancy instruments, that the thrust of the Galilean revolution issued.

It is not to be construed from the above sketch that nothing happened between the Aristotelian mechanics of the thirteenth century and Galileo. Changes took place during this period that anticipated and helped what Galileo was later to expound. But these preliminary urges for change were to culminate in Galileo's concerted effort, which completed the conceptual about-face. At any rate, a similar conceptual reorientation has not taken place in sociology, and without such a fundamental change in the intellectual outlook, refinement in the formal aspect of an explanation and elaborate use of numbers, including mathematics and what passes for measurement, are window dressings, which do not help the business of verifying a theory. As a matter of fact, mere sophistication in these operations tends to make them only esoteric and to confuse people without producing explanations that can withstand empirical tests.

Sociological Explanations

Examples of sociological explanation are presented in the next three chapters for the purpose of bringing out the difficulties embedded in the foundation of modern sociology. These are taken from what I consider to be the mainstream of current sociology. This is not, of course, a comprehensive survey. Nor are the dangers of oversimplification entirely avoided in the course of condensing the relevant arguments. The focus is on the style of explanation rather than the content. Attempts at empirical generalizations in sociology, of which there are meager beginnings, are not considered, since these have not yet been incorporated into current sociological thinking to any significant extent.

VI. Understanding Capi[

M Y FIRST example is the celebrated explanation of how modern capitalism came about—by the German sociologist Max Weber (1864–1920). Weber has had a great influence on modern sociology in terms of the concepts he formulated and the manner in which he used them. He expounded and practiced what might be called interpretative sociology, or sociology of understanding, which holds that it is not enough for sociology to explain a social phenomenon by showing that it follows as a logical consequence from empirically verifiable statements of facts, or from assumptions of a theoretical nature that are consistent with known empirical observations. Weber maintained that this form of explanation is meaningful only if it can be related to our subjective experiences; that is, only if it produces the kind of understanding that comes from shared experiences. It is perhaps a laudable policy to put the flesh of intuitive understanding on the explanatory skeleton, provided that the explanation itself meets the criteria of science. But it is, strictly speaking, a nonscientific desideratum. Furthermore, the pursuit of this goal has created a mystique of understanding that preempts the development of scientifically adequate explanations, and, as a consequence, has arrested the growth of sociology as a science.

Weber's treatise on capitalism has been challenged on factual grounds, but without the challenges really making a dent in it as a sociological theory, for both Weber's and his revisionists' arguments are peculiarly insulated from crucial tests of an empirical nature. And it is not likely that there will be decisive evidence

„ainst Weber's thesis within his own framework, for this
..es with it its own criteria of validity, which are essentially
nonscientific. The following is a reconstruction of Weber's explanation of capitalism taken from his famous *The Protestant
Ethic and the Spirit of Capitalism* and other writings on the sociology of religion.

1.

The motive force for the development of capitalism, according to Weber, is the attitude that underlies this form of economic activity, or the spirit of capitalism. By capitalism is to be
understood an economic activity directed toward profit making
and pursued with objective means, freed from traditions governing the rate of profit, the amount of work, and the relationship
to workers and customers. Its distinctive features are the use of
capital, systematic bookkeeping, and above all, control and organization of free labor. The spirit of capitalism is characterized
by a philosophy of material accumulation, in the service of
which are extolled the virtues of honesty, industry, punctuality,
and frugality. Capitalism grows out of a psychological climate in
which the pursuit of profit for its own sake is accepted as the
proper goal of life. The spirit of capitalism, which embodies this
attitude, together with a code of ethics, is not an adaptation to
or a simple effect of a capitalist economy, which might develop
as a result of changing material conditions. It is rather a necessary ingredient, if not a clear-cut cause, of modern capitalism.
This assertion is far from being an undisputed statement of fact
among sociologists and economic historians. Weber justifies it by
observing that in the prosperous proto-capitalistic economies
that did not develop into full-fledged capitalism, as, for example,
the flourishing enterprises of Renaissance Italy, this spirit of capitalism was lacking; but it was clearly a way of life in the relatively poor colonies of seventeenth-century English America,
which were later to create the most accomplished form of modern capitalism. At any rate, given this relationship, Weber's task

is to explain it, especially in view of the fact that material possession had been frowned upon in the religious teachings of the West, the unique breeding-ground of capitalism.

The first step in the explanation of this historical phenomenon is the relationship between the religious precepts of Puritanism, especially Calvinism, and the spirit of capitalism. On the one hand, the Calvinists held that the world existed for the glorification of God and that it was man's duty to fulfil this purpose by carrying out mundane tasks with diligence. The Calvinists saw themselves as active tools of God's will. On the other hand, they also believed in the doctrine of predestination, according to which a man's salvation was absolutely predetermined by God and nothing that he might do on earth could change the status of his salvation. Men of this faith were, consequently, spurred on to toil continually at the work of their calling as a means of escaping from the faithless doubt concerning their salvation. This stricture was sometimes interpreted even to mean that work was a way to salvation and that God helped those who helped themselves. Along with this exhortation to work, the Puritans were warned against idleness and even against the enjoyment of the fruits of their toil. Work was the duty of the poor and the rich alike, and it had to be continued without wasting time in relaxation and merriment.

Now there is an obvious affinity, Weber would say, between the way of life prescribed by the teachings of the Puritans and the mode of behavior characteristic of modern capitalism, and it makes sense that they should go hand in hand, if not being causally related to each other. It is particularly understandable, so the argument would run, that the combined effect of hard work and abstention from the enjoyment of material possessions should result in the accumulation and reinvestment of wealth, which are so basic to early capitalist growth.

This relationship between Puritanism and the spirit of capitalism is deducible from more general principles concerning religion and daily activity, especially economic behavior. On the one hand, to the extent that a religion is rational in the sense that it is free of magical elements, including miracles and mysticism, and that the religious beliefs are integrated with an understanding of worldly happenings, religious precepts have a measure of influence on the daily activity of men. On the other hand, the character of a religion with regard to rationality is very much dependent on the life style of the people who promote and practice the religion. In general, artisans, traders, and entrepreneurs, collectively referred to as the civic strata by Weber, are conditioned by their way of life, which is based on technical and commercial activities. The religion of this group, as a consequence, in common with that of the intellectual stratum, tends to be rational, being relatively free of magic and embodying a code of ethics guiding the behavior of man in this world.

The root religions of the West have been initiated and supported by the civic strata. This is true, in the main, of Judaism and Islam, the latter beginning as a religion of warriors and later becoming allied with the petty bourgeoisie. Christianity, in particular, began as a religion of artisans and, to a large extent, remained tied to city dwellers throughout its history. This is in contrast to the religions of the East: Confucianism, a religion of gentlemen scholars; Hinduism, of a privileged caste of *literati;* and Buddhism, of world-rejecting monks. Confucianism was a highly rationalized religion, having been founded by intellectuals, and, as might be expected, worked itself into the very fabric of the secular Chinese ethical system. But it lacked the philosophy of activism that has characterized the religions of the West, especially Calvinism.

Thus the influence of Calvinism on the spirit of capitalism is to be explained in terms of the rationality of its theology. As a matter of fact, the reason why Catholicism and even Lutheranism did not have the same influence on the development of capitalism is precisely that they did not achieve the degree of rationalism that Calvinism did. The Catholics retained vestiges of magic, notably in the functions of the priest who acted as an intermediary between man and God, and for them the good work that gained them merit in the eyes of God was not the kind that required a systematic organization of everyday life. For the Lutherans, the notion of calling was important, but a calling to them meant something about which the individual had no choice and which was not interpreted as necessarily entailing worldly activity. Calvinists, by contrast, thought of a calling as a chosen work of a practical nature at which man is enjoined to labor hard. Calvinism, the most rationalized religion of the world, carried a message of activism.

Schematically then: (1) a rationalized religion has practical consequences for the everyday behavior of the believer; (2) the character of a religion is influenced by its bearers; (3) the religion of the civic strata (the bourgeois element) tends to be sober and practical; (4) the religions of the West, especially Christianity, have been, by and large, allied with, if not founded by, the civic strata; (5) Calvinism is the most rationalized of the Christian doctrines and has a strong activist cast. From these it follows, more or less deductively, that (6) the ethical system of Calvinism has a strong influence on the conduct of man, including of course, economic behavior.

2.

But Weber's analysis thus far does not explain, in the deductive sense discussed in the preceding section, why the Calvinist doctrine should produce any *particular* effect on economic behavior; that is, why it should be responsible for the flourishing of *capitalism*. To be sure, there is an affinity between the exhortations to work hard and the prohibition of enjoyment of life and waste of time, on the one hand, and profit seeking, accumulation and reinvestment of capital, and the virtues of honesty, industry, frugality, and punctuality, on the other. But these two sets of characteristics are by no means identical. Besides, it is not self-evident why the Calvinists' virtues should necessarily lead to the rational principle of economic organization that is supposed to be characteristic of capitalism, as for example, control and organization of free labor. Weber's ostensible purpose in his extensive inquiries concerning religion and economy was to ascertain the psychological predisposition which originates in religious beliefs and practices and which influences man's behavior in other spheres of life. But he did not explain the connection between one set of factors and the other; that is, he did not derive this connection from more general principles. He merely suggested what meaning Calvinist teachings had to the believer in terms of how he would relate to his goal and available means. Assuming that the overriding goal of the Calvinist was the salvation of his soul, the Calvinist theology imparted to the faithful a certain meaning relevant to the acquisition of attitudes impelling him to action. Weber apparently relied upon common sense to fathom the meaning the Calvinist doctrine might have had for the Puritan saints, the meaning that was translated into action. Weber's recurrent use of such phrases as "it is understandable," "as is well known," "it is easy to understand," etc., is indicative of his attempts to establish intuitively meaningful connections between beliefs and behavior.

The relationship between a man's assessment of the situation he finds himself in and his behavior is at the foundation of Weber's sociology. A man who sees the situation as requiring hard work and frugal living for the salvation of his soul manifests rational economic behavior, the epitome of which is the capitalistic enterprise. Weber resorts to this principle not only for connecting Calvinism and capitalism, but also for establishing the would-be empirical generalizations from which this connection might be, at least partly, deduced. For example, Weber says that it is understandable why the religion of the civic strata should be oriented toward practicality. Here again, Weber's analysis is in terms of how the members of the civic strata, say, artisans, view their relationship to the world as men of practical affairs and how the meaning they attach to the situation influences the cosmology that they adopt. Consequently what might appear to be empirical generalizations, such as that the rationality of a religion exerts influence on everyday life, only partially depend on empirical observation. The validity of Weber's explanation thus is very much tied to the problems of interpreting what meaning a man gives to the situation and how this meaning is related to his conduct.

Weber was apparently wary of investigating the workings of this relationship, regarding it as a psychological problem. But unless this relationship is clarified, the principle that presumably explains a complex of behavior called capitalism does not explain anything. It is not different, in this regard, from the Aristotelian explanation that bodies fall because of their gravity (heaviness). Neither the Weberian concept of subjective meaning of the situation nor the Aristotelian concept of gravity allows us to make predictions that can be tested against observations; they merely give us tautologies—heavy bodies fall by their nature, and a situation that is perceived to call for rational behavior produces rational behavior.

3.

A man's assessment of the situation relevant to his behavior, what might be called his orientation, has been elaborated upon by Weber's American disciple, Talcott Parsons. According to Parsons, a man's orientation can be mentally separated into four components, which he calls "pattern variables." Each pattern variable has two opposite poles, like positive and negative electric charges, and a man's orientation to a situation is characterized by the combination of these pattern variable poles that he chooses. The pattern variables are named in terms of these poles. They are "universalism-particularism," "affectivity-affective neutrality," "diffuseness-specificity," "quality-performance." The first dichotomy has to do with the choice between applying a code of behavior to everybody uniformly and objectively (universalism) and making exceptions in the application of the code for special considerations, such as kinship ties (particularism). The second pattern variable of "affectivity-affective neutrality" evolves around the choice between regarding the situation as an end in itself for the purpose of venting one's own emotion or gratifying one's appetite (affectivity), and regarding it as a means to some other ends and checking emotional release or immediate gratification (affective neutrality). The dichotomy making up the third pattern variable, "diffuseness-specificity," has to do with the scope of orientation. If a man attaches significance to a segmental aspect of the situation, especially in dealing with other human beings (as in business transactions as opposed to familial relations), the orientation is specific; otherwise it is diffuse. The last pattern variable of "quality-performance" involves the choice between evaluating a situation for "what it is" (quality) and for "what it does" (performance), or in terms of relationships involving another person, between "who he is" and "what he does." A mother's relationship to her child, for instance, is particularistic, affective, diffuse, and quality-oriented.

In terms of these pattern variables, Weber's thesis concerning the relationship between Calvinism and Protestantism might be restated with a little more substance. The Calvinist theology inculcated attitudes that are characterizable by universalism, affective neutrality, specificity, and performance, and these are exactly the pattern variable poles underlying the economic behavior known as capitalism. Now the questions concerning the validity of this thesis boil down to: Did Calvinism really produce the attitudes of universalism, affective neutrality, specificity, and performance? Is capitalistic economic activity characterizable by the same pattern variable poles? And, more generally, do attitudes regularly produce behavioral effects that are similarly characterizable in terms of pattern variables?

This last is a crucial question for sociology as a science, for a successful answer to it will lead to an empirical generalization, without which there can be no theory, no explanation. The problems having to do with how attitudes get inculcated and how they in turn affect behavior have proved difficult to handle in social psychology. But even leaving aside the notion of attitude, if we are to establish the correlation between one system of behavior, say religious practices, and another, such as economic activity, in terms of the pattern variables, there must be practical and unambiguous criteria of how to recognize human behavior that is universalistic or particularistic, affective or affectively neutral, etc. Such practical criteria are also needed in order to establish the pattern variable contents of the historical events, Calvinism and capitalism. It is to be remembered that the pattern variables refer to how a person perceives the situation, what meaning he gives to it. They refer to an internal state, to use graphic if inaccurate language, which is not observable. (It is inaccurate, because the meaning that we give to a situation is neither inside nor outside our body, no more than a figment of the imagination is internal to us.) It we are to gauge this state merely by introspecting how we, as sensitive human beings, would perceive the situation, we must give up all pretenses to an objective science. The problem becomes compounded if we are to interpret not only concrete actions of men in specific situations but also the teachings of a religious group or a code of ethics. It is one thing to say that my behavior in my lawyer's office at nine o'clock this morning was universalistic, affectively neutral, and so forth, in the sense that I made these choices of orientation (assuming that such an introspection is possible and reliable), but it is quite another story to apply these adjectives to the writings of John Calvin or Benjamin Franklin.

The use of a subjective concept, such as situational meaning, poses a fundamental problem for sociology as an objective science. The problem is the same whether the "meaning" is characterized as rationality à la Weber or analyzed into Parsons' pattern variables; these merely sort out the various elements of the "meaning," but again in subjective terms. The concepts of pattern variables, however, have the advantage of making it crystal clear that the mode of analysis in Weber's and Parsons' sociology is in terms of how we think a man, the actor, looks out at the world. In the course of developing the notions of pattern variables, Parsons bares the basic approach of interpretative sociology, which is essentially subjective, or phenomenological.

Weber's sociology of understanding, which is explicitly,

though not very clearly, expounded in his methodological writings, has permeated aspects of modern sociology. This circumstance, at least in America, is largely due to Parsons, who was instrumental in introducing Weber's writings and propagating his mode of analysis. Weber's influence in current sociological practices, of course, goes beyond Parsonian sociology. In fact, sociology of understanding itself, with which Weber's name is associated, is an expression of the familiar and pervasive notion that things have a purpose that can be understood in introspective terms. Weber's sociology is an elaborate effort to make a systematic application of this common sense view to social phenomena, as Aristole's cosmology was a systematic recasting of the world in the same common sense framework. The difficulties in Weber's explanation of the rise of capitalism discussed in this chapter, therefore, derive from a thought-habit more general than Weber's conceptual scheme. But to the considerable extent that Weber's sociology is regarded as the conceptual foundation of sociology and his methodology of understanding, with all its ambiguities, is taken as a guide to sociological analysis, *the Weberian heritage in modern sociology must be regarded as an obstacle to scientific sociology.*

VII. The Function
of Social Inequalities

WHAT IS called "functional analysis" has been much in use in modern sociology and has even been equated to sociological explanation itself by some sociologists. Despite this claim for exclusiveness on the part of sociologists, however, a variety of functional theories have been employed in other sciences—in biology, psychology, and anthropology—and have been discussed and criticized by both philosophers and scientists. A typical functional theory explains a phenomenon by asserting that it contributes to the survival or well-being of the whole, a system of which it is a part. In principle, there is no reason why satisfactory scientific theories that meet the criteria of testability cannot be constructed from this general idea. In practice, however, the functional theories so far developed in sociology have failed to meet the scientific criteria, though perhaps imparting understanding of sorts to those who believe in them. The problems of functional analysis have been discussed from the point of view of logic and testability, as well as in terms of the psychological reasons for their plausibility and moral implications. My purpose here is to examine a typical functional theory in sociology in the light of these problems and to consider how an uncritical dependence on immature functional theories has retarded the growth of sociology as a science.

1.

There is a much-debated explanation of why there are differences in the "prestige" and "esteem" that men enjoy in a society. This theory was formulated by two eminent leaders of American sociology, Kingsley Davis and Wilbert Moore, and was later revised and set forth in Davis' *Human Society*. Prestige, according to Davis, is an "invidious value" attached to the positions that a person holds, and transferred to the holder himself. According to this definition, two persons who occupy the same position have the same "prestige." But depending on the conduct of the incumbents of the same position, one may have more "esteem" than the other. Esteem is a valuation that a man's behavior places on the person.

These are commonly accepted definitions in sociology. The explanation to be presented below assumes that this differentiation of prestige and esteem is an empirical fact. It is indeed thought to be present in every society. Although social stratification is defined in this theory to include both prestige and esteem, the latter aspect is all but ignored in the explanatory scheme. In order not to leave an unnecessary gap in the model explanation to be considered and yet not wishing to supply the missing links myself, I will not consider the esteem aspect of social stratification. This omission makes no difference for the present purpose, which is not to discuss the content of the theory but its methodology.

The functional explanation for this allegedly universal phenomenon begins as follows: Some positions are more important than others for the survival of a society, or for its proper functioning as a going concern, and some require more talent and/or training on the part of the incumbents. Rewards are attached to positions to induce "people to seek the positions and fulfil the essential duties." In general the positions that are "the most important" and require "the greatest" talent and/or training carry "the best rewards." In brief, there is differentiation of rewards associated with positions in any society. According to Davis and Moore, social stratification is defined as inequality in the prestige of positions resulting from differentiated rewards. It can therefore be concluded that there is social stratification in any society.

So far, however, this is not a functional analysis of social stratification, since it does not tell us what significance the differentiation of rewards has for the survival or proper functioning of a society. Davis and Moore go on to state that "social inequality is thus an unconsciously evolved device by which societies insure that the most important positions are conscientiously filled by the most qualified persons." What is implied here is that filling the most important positions by the most qualified persons—call this the principle of "optimal allocation of personnel" to save our breath—is a necessary condition for the survival or well-being of a society. Davis and Moore do not state this explicitly, but unless this principle is a necessity, the statement that "societies insure" this effect is meaningless, and no functional explanation emerges from it.

The Davis-Moore theory, with this implicit postulate as part of it, then, might be said to explain, in the scientific sense, the fact of social stratification as a universal phenomenon and hence its presence in a particular society at a particular time. But this would depend on how we interpret the assertion that societies insure that the most qualified fill the most important positions by social stratification. For example, the fact that there is social stratification in the present-day United States, assuming for the moment that this is the case, might be explained by deducing this statement from the theory, which is schematically presented below in terms of the bare essentials: (1) Optimal allocation of personnel is a necessary condition for the survival (or proper functioning) of a society, which is to say, if there is a properly functioning society, one may be sure that the most important positions are occupied by the most qualified persons. (2) Social stratification insures an optimal allocation of personnel. (3) In the United States today, there is a properly functioning society.

Now, whether or not the statement that there is social stratification in the United States today logically follows from these depends on how one interprets the proposition that "social stratification insures optimal allocation of personnel." If it simply means, as it seems to, that if social stratification is present, optimal allocation of personnel will invariably ensue, that is, that the former is a sufficient condition for the latter, the fact of social stratification does not follow from the theory. (Just as, from the proposition that if it rains on an open pavement the pavement will get wet and the assertion that the pavement is now wet, it does not follow that it has rained; the pavement might have been sprinkled with a hose.) In order for the theory to explain this fact, that is, for the latter to be deduced as a logical consequence of the former—this is what we mean by saying that the former explains the latter—social stratification must be understood to mean a necessary condition of optimal allocation of personnel. That is, the proposition in question must be understood to mean that the only way to achieve an optimal allocation of personnel is by social stratification. This, in conjunction with the functional importance of allocating the most qualified to the most important positions for the well-being of a society, is tantamount to saying that social inequality is inevitable for the survival, or well-being, of a society.

It might be possible to circumvent the inevitability principle and yet come up with a logically satisfactory explanation of social stratification. In particular, social stratification might be thought of as one of the ways by which optimal allocation of personnel is brought about: that is, the former might be postulated as a sufficient, rather than a necessary, condition for the latter. But in this case, optimal allocation of personnel implies alternatives to social stratification, and from the facts that a society is functioning well and therefore that its members are properly placed, it cannot be deduced that social stratification exists. An explanation constructed along these lines can only lead to the "trivial" conclusion that social stratification is a possible means of producing a well-functioning society, but not *why* it actually exists, this last point being the objective of the functional explanation.

The Davis-Moore theory has been correctly assessed as implying the inevitability thesis and attacked on ideological grounds. In reply, Davis did not, unfortunately, throw any more

light on how the proposition that social stratification insures optimal allocation of personnel should be interpreted. Instead, he
argued that it is not possible to prove or disprove the inevitability thesis, thus side-stepping the issue. In the sense that a proposition in a theory sometimes cannot be directly verified by itself,
Davis' contention is, of course, correct. For instance, the
assumption that molecules travel in a straight line at a constant
speed, which is part of the kinetic theory of gases, is not directly
verifiable by itself. But to the extent that a whole theory can,
and must, be verified by checking empirically observable consequences predicted from the theory, any proposition forming
part of it is indirectly falsified or confirmed (in a restricted
sense). In this light, Davis' disclaimer does not absolve him of
the scientific responsibility to make his assumptions explicit. It
appears to me that he cannot propose his theory as a nontrivial
explanation of social stratification without upholding its inevitability as a functional necessity. The justification for such a stand,
from a scientific point of view, must be derived from the predictive power of the theory that embodies it, not from an ideological prejudice.

But the functional explanation of social stratification has not
yielded empirically testable predictions. This is partly due to the
very ambiguity surrounding the inevitability issue just discussed.
Sociologists have been inclined, by and large, to the view that
socially necessary functions can be fulfilled in general by
different means in different physical and cultural environments.
Thus Davis' noncommittal stand concerning the inevitability of
social stratification can be thought of as a special manifestation
of the functionalist dilemma. One horn of this dilemma is a
cultural pluralism which postulates functional alternatives and
thus leads to a theory that gives only "trivial" explanations, and
the other is the requirement of a strong explanation which entails cultural absolutism, sometimes with ideologically unpalatable implications, such as that social inequality is inevitable.
Consequently, functional analysis in sociology has given us much
pseudo-explanation and few scientifically useful predictions. But

there are other reasons why functional analysis has been barren of fruitful hypotheses in sociology, and as long as these reasons hold, asserting the inevitability of social stratification alone will not make the Davis-Moore theory more useful. I now turn to these other problems.

2.

The first problem to be considered has to do with the uncertain empirical identity of the phenomenon to be explained, which is, in this instance, social stratification. This problem is of course not peculiar to functional analysis. It is, in fact, so typical of sociological explanations built upon impressionistic generalities and incompletely thought-out speculative ideas that it might be worthwhile discussing it here at the risk of making the focus of this chapter somewhat diffuse. Despite the fact that the concept of social stratification is one of the most frequently used in sociology, there is no universally accepted definition by which the strata (social classes) can be empirically delineated and their respective members identified. More surprisingly, even within a single explanatory scheme the concept is often not given a clearly consistent definition, as will be shown presently for the case of Davis and Moore.

In the above schematized chain of deductions constituting the functional explanation of social stratification in the present-day United States, there are two statements referring to ostensibly observable phenomena: one, that there is social stratification, and the other, that there is a well-functioning society—both in the present-day United States. These two statements must be empirically verifiable if the explanation is to have any meaning. The first statement is, of course, the one to be explained. If we are to test the theory by making a prediction, say that there is social stratification in Communist China, from the Davis-Moore theory, together with an empirical assertion that Communist China is a going concern, again, this assertion as well as the prediction must be empirically verifiable. There are features in the Davis-Moore theory that prevent this possibility.

In the functional theory of social stratification under consideration, social stratification is defined explicitly in terms of positions rather than persons; namely, social stratification is the unequal distribution of rewards and prestige among different positions that persons occupy. But the text of the explanation inconsistently refers to social stratification of persons. First of all, what are positions? Davis speaks of a position of a person as his identity. Being a male is a position, being a forty-year-old is a position, being a carpenter is a position, being a head carpenter in X shop is a position, and so forth. These positions of a person get combined into a station. In Davis' formulation, the positions that "tend to adhere together" to define his generalized position, and "the sum total of one's major positions" are referred to as his station. "Thus, doctor, lawyer, and professor are each different occupational positions, but are on about the same level of evaluation and accompanied by similar allied positions. A common name, 'professions,' designating a station is, therefore, given the incumbents." Stations in turn help define strata. A stratum is "a mass of persons," a division of a population "enjoying roughly the same station."

Finally, social stratification: "Any population is commonly divided into strata. In fact, specifying the strata is one of the most convenient and frequently used ways of giving a shorthand description of a social structure. Such a procedure implies the existence of relative rank. Different stations are felt to be unequal in the public estimation and hence a hierarchy of strata is recognized." "The best known types [of stratification] are the caste system . . . and the open class system . . ." And, "When we think of castes and classes, and of social stratification in general, we have in mind groups who occupy different positions in the social order and enjoy different amounts of prestige." This last quote and others in the same vein, implying that prestige accrues to people, are inconsistent with the concept of social stratification defined in terms of positions rather than persons. Thus it is unclear whether the phenomenon to be explained is that different persons enjoy different amounts of prestige due to their

positions or stations, or that different positions and stations carry
different amounts of prestige. This lack of clarity, of course,
makes it difficult to empirically ascertain the content of the
statement that there is social stratification in the United States
today.

For the purpose of present discussion, it will simplify the matter, without doing injustice to the spirit of the Davis-Moore
theory, to equate occupations with stations. Then we may understand from the above quotes that there are divisions or classes of
stations entailing different amounts of prestige. And the division
can be understood to be based on similarities in the stations and
defined independently of prestige. With this interpretation,
then, to verify, for example, that social stratification exists in the
United States today, we must first identify these strata and then
determine their respective prestige. But despite our feelings and
vague impressions that such strata exist as distinguishable entities, their identities are empirically indeterminate. For example,
what occupations are "professions" and what stratum do they
belong to? Are public accountants professionals? Are social
workers? Nurses? Realtors? Call girls? It might be that clusters
of occupations can be defined in terms of similarities in their
positions or social attributes by some empirical and objective
method, but such clusters have not been defined except impres-
sionistically and inconsistently.

We may ignore the notion of social stratum for the moment
and think of social stratification simply in terms of inequalities
in occupational prestige, taking occupations singly, a practice
implied in some contexts in which this term is used in the
Davis-Moore analysis. This procedure has been adopted in empirical social research. But when occupations are thus taken singly,
there are practical difficulties in determining the respective prestige accorded them by the popular estimate, which are not
trivial. The United States Department of Labor listed over
20,000 jobs (and over 40,000 job titles) in 1949, only a fraction
of which can be meaningfully discriminated in terms of prestige
by any one person. For this reason, and technical ones that need

not detain us here, it has been possible to assess the prestige of only a handful of occupations that are meaningful to the public. The upshot of the research in this area is that only a small number—about a dozen—of occupations can be ordered by prestige, and that there are several such hierarchies which cannot be combined into a unified system. The prestige ratings of close to a hundred occupations have been devised, but the procedure followed here is more or less arbitrary, resembling the proceedings of beauty contests. But, indeed, the rating of the beauty contestants and the eventual ranking of the finalists into the queen and the first and the second runners-up have a more determinate meaning than these prestige ratings of occupations. Occupations are abstractions, and the notion of prestige is more nebulous than that of beauty. It may not be any easier to define beauty in words than prestige, but it is less difficult to perceive the beauty of a girl in the flesh relative to another than to decide which of two occupations, say actor or sportsman, is more prestigious. "Actor" here does not refer to a single person, nor to a determinate number of persons. The same is true of "sportsman." This is one major reason why it is difficult to show a hierarchy of occupational prestige by an objective method even for a handful of occupations.

Due to these considerations, it must be concluded that if social stratification exists in the United States today, it is at best partial and segmentalized. This conclusion is in contradiction to Davis' assertion that the social strata into which a society is divided are ranked, or that "all positions carry a certain prestige, either high or low." Since this is the fact the Davis-Moore theory is supposed to explain, it looks as though the purpose of the explanation is vitiated. It is as if a theory were constructed to explain why unicorns have single horns, or why man has free will. The phenomenon to be explained has only an impressionistic, not to say imaginary, existence, much as did Aristotle's crystalline spheres embedded with stars.

Social stratification is not a fact to be taken for granted but a conception of society implying certain empirical relationships among social elements, whether these be individuals or positions occupied by the individuals; it is truly an hypothesis to be tested. "Self-evident truths," such as that man's behavior is goal-oriented, figure prominently as explanatory principles in sociology, a circumstance making it difficult to put sociological explanations on firm empirical grounds. But the hollowness of the sociological enterprise today is never so evident as when a poorly identified phenomenon is asserted to be universal and an elaborate verbal structure is constructed to explain it, as in the Davis-Moore explanation of social stratification.

3.

The supposedly empirical statement that the United States is today a going concern, which is crucial in the above heuristic example of functional explanation, has other problems that are typical of and peculiar to functional analysis.

That social stratification is a necessary condition for the survival of a society, which the functional theory is bound to assert as a satisfactory explanatory principle, implies that a society without stratification is either dead, sick, or a nonsociety. Suppose then that we come across a communal farm of "hippie" families, who sustain themselves by working on the farm and sharing what they produce and reproduce themselves by bearing children like any other people. Such communities have actually sprung up in the United States and other countries recently. Now if we should find no stratification (in the sense of differential prestige attached to positions) in this community, can we conclude that the functional theory is thereby disconfirmed? Or, to go back to the situation in the present-day United States, on the basis of the conclusion that there is no evidence of the kind of social stratification that Davis and Moore seem to have in mind, can we claim that the functional theory is invalidated? In the first case, we might be inclined to say that the "hippie" community is sick, if not dead, or even that it is really not a society. These arguments could well be made to save the theory, because the terms "society," "survival," "functioning well," are not given empirically determinate criteria in the theory. In the second case we would be more reluctant to say that the society in which we live is dead, not a going concern, or a nonsociety. We would probably say, instead, that there is really social stratification but we just don't know how to show it. (If one were persistent in demanding objective evidence of social stratification, he would be considered absurd, since "everybody knows there are social classes in the United States.") In either event the theory is protected from possible falsification and not testable. But a theory that is empirically not testable is of no scientific value.

It is a typical feature of functional theories in sociology that the whole to which the phenomenon of interest is to contribute is not clearly specified. This whole is, of course, often a society, which, unlike a country—a political unit—is difficult enough to identify in practical terms. But it is sometimes referred to as a social system instead of society, which makes it even more difficult to pin it down as an empirical entity. Nor are definite criteria given as to when a social system is viable. Expressions such as "adequately functioning," "well adapted," as well as "survival" or "going concern," are used to convey this notion, but it is seldom stated in specific terms as to when a social system is or is not functioning properly. In this respect, a functional proposition in sociology does not have the advantages that its would-be counterparts in biology do. For example, it may be said that the human heart has the function of circulating the blood, and that blood circulation is indispensable for the maintenance of human life. Here we can specify what a human being is, when he is dead, and, with a reasonable determinateness, when he is or is not functioning properly. We can, of course, also tell when there is or there is not a heart in a person's body at a given time. Thus, a functional explanation of the human heart, if we were to propound it, would be based on a testable theory.

Despite this testability, however, the functional theory of the heart just constructed along the line of reasoning pursued in the functional theory of social stratification reveals a peculiar weakness of the functional explanation. If we are to understand from the theory that the heart is necessary for blood circulation, as social stratification is understood to be a necessary condition for an optimal allocation of personnel, this theory is about to be falsified, since artificial hearts are being developed in medical laboratories. Even if artificial hearts should not work out, there are obviously competing theories that do not take the human heart as a necessary condition for human survival, in spite of the fact that it is a universal phenomenon. These competing theories, whatever their content, can only explain how the heart works, or what it does, but not why it exists. The difference between this and what a functional theory seeks to explain is in saying that the heart circulates the blood and saying that it circulates the blood, therefore it exists. The latter explains the existence of the heart; the former does not. Thus the functional theory of the human heart modeled after the Davis-Moore social stratification theory helps reveal the answers that a functional theory in sociology gives to "why" questions and thereby points to the underlying habit of thinking.

4.

An empirical generalization that is built into theories, or a scientific law, asserts the regularity with which two things, properties, or events are connected to each other. This is an essential characteristic of all scientific laws in the simplest form, although more than two things, properties, or events may be involved in more complex cases. Scientific laws are of the form: "Man is mortal"; "Ice floats in water"; "Heavy bodies fall." There is a species of scientific law that brings in the notion of time and establishes an invariable sequence of things or events. For example: "Heating an ice cube in a pan results in the ice cube melting"; "A fall from the top of a twenty-story building results in fatal injuries"; "Oral deprivation in childhood produces neurosis in later life"; "Rubbing two sticks of wood together vigorously produces smoke and fire." Generalizations of this kind which form part of deductively arranged theories are called causal laws. A contingent statement concerning a sequence of particular things or events at a particular time interval that can be subsumed under a causal law specifies the cause and the effect in the sequence. For instance, when a man dies after falling from a twenty-story building, we say that the fall caused the man's death, the effect. Or, when we see a neurotic person who was deprived of oral gratification in his childhood, we say, rightly or wrongly, that the oral deprivation is the cause of his neurosis. In these instances, as is usually the case in causal statements, the cause gives a sufficient condition for the effect. But sometimes a necessary as well as sufficient condition for the effect is given by the cause, as when we say that the tubercle bacillus is the cause of tuberculosis.

Now, it is an undeniable fact that many things and events in nature are observed in time sequence, and they are coupled in the sense that whenever one occurs the other also occurs (sufficient condition) and/or that without one, the other does not occur (necessary condition). Things and events that are produced by man have this characteristic relationship to human action. I throw a stone in the water, and it is invariably followed by spreading ripples. I rub two sticks together and fire results, not so invariably but regularly enough to make the effort worthwhile if I had no other way of making fire. It is thus easy to think of natural phenomena as being produced, or caused, by some human-like agents. It is a plausible conjecture that the causal way of looking at the world is an extension of the mental habit that we acquired in observing the influence of our action on the things that surround us. The belief in the spirits that inhabit the primitive and not so primitive worlds and control man and his environment alike derives from the same source. This outlook on the natural world, which is called animism, is ingrained in our common sense, and expressions in our everyday language betray this. The Aristotelian way of explaining the world and what happens in it, in terms of agents that cause the phenomena, was animistic.

One can think of causal laws and causal explanations strictly in terms of their logical properties, i.e., as conjunctions of events and things connected in time, one preceding the other as a sufficient or a sufficient and necessary condition of the other, without introducing, implicitly or explicitly, the notion of a human-like agent. Such relationships are useful in scientific discourse as a convenient way of stating a special kind of empirical regularity of theoretical import. Especially in applied fields where science is used to control events, the causal mode of thinking is indispensable. If, for example, we wish to increase the yield of our land, we must identify the sufficient condition for soil fertility that we can apply in advance of harvest. Or, if we wish to prevent the scourge of cancer, we must isolate a not only sufficient but also necessary condition for the development of cancer and apply the knowledge before the disease sets in. Consequently, causal analysis is prevalent in sciences closely allied to practical affairs. Except for this practical consideration, however, science could perhaps get along without causal laws, though rendered somewhat ineloquent. But there is a danger of seeing human-like agents in causes, or giving special epistemological significance to causal relations because they resemble the way human beings produce events or things. This danger is especially great in areas where the regularities of natural events are stated in terms of vague abstractions, as in sociology and formerly also in biology. That the popularity of causal thinking is at least partly due to this kind of human analogy can perhaps be seen by the fact that causal laws are sought after more avidly in fields that deal with human beings, namely, biology, psychology, anthropology, and sociology.

The animistic undertow of causal thinking is most acutely felt in teleological explanations. A teleological statement is a special kind of causal proposition in which what is conceived to be the effect in a sequence of events precedes the cause in time. The cause in a teleological statement is commonly called the "purpose," "goal," or "function." When "why" questions elicit a "purpose" or a "goal" as answers, we have teleological explanations. For example: "I turned on the radio to listen to the news"; "My wife went out to buy a fan"; "My neighbor sprinkles his lawn every day to make the grass grow." In these instances, "listening to the news," "buying a fan," and "making the grass grow," events that have not yet taken place, are given as reasons for, respectively, "turning on the radio," "going out," and "sprinkling the lawn," events that have already taken place or are in progress. These function satisfactorily as explanations by presupposing implicit generalizations of the form: "Listening to the news (on the radio)" implies turning on the radio. "Buying fans" implies going out. "Making grass grow" implies sprinkling the lawn. If the first generalization is based on empirical regularities, obviously, "listening to the news" is a sufficient condition for turning on the radio. (There are other reasons for listening to a radio, but if one wishes to listen to the news on the radio, a radio must be turned on.) And similarly "buying fans" and "making the grass grow" are sufficient conditions for "going out" and "sprinkling the lawn," respectively.

How, it might be asked, can an event that has not taken place cause a temporally antecedent event, since by definition the cause precedes the effect? This obvious difficulty can be avoided by saying that what causes the past or present behavior of myself, my wife, or my neighbor is not the as yet unrealized results of our respective behavior, but our intentions to produce these effects. Intentions "clearly" precede action, and, therefore, if we understand intentions by "purposes" or "goals" in teleological statements, these are proper causal statements. But only human beings and human-like things—gods, spirits, demons, etc.—have intentions; and when we apply teleological statements to nonhuman things, we have animism.

As has been seen, functional theories in sociology explain a social phenomenon by postulating as a sufficient condition the societal survival of well-being (which is the function or the goal

of the social occurrence in question). The blatantly anthropo-
morphic word "purpose" does not often appear in functionalists'
discussions, but, in these, the spirit of animism is only thinly
disguised. In the following passages, for example, Davis speaks
of society as if it were a human being, and thereby reveals the
significance that functional explanation has for his way of thinking. "One may ask what kind of rewards a society has at its
disposal in distributing its personnel and securing essential services." "Social inequality is thus an unconsciously evolved device by which societies insure that the most important positions
are conscientiously filled by the most qualified persons." Or,
"Actually a society does not need to reward positions in proportion to their functional importance."

From the above discussion, it must not be construed that
future events cannot be a sufficient condition for present or past
events or things, nor that a statement which asserts such a relationship is necessarily animistic. The point to be gained is that a
scientific law merely establishes, within the context of a theory,
regularities between events or things, and, from the point of
view of scientific utility, it makes no difference whether the
temporally antecedent or consequent event or thing is the
sufficient condition. Thus, teleological generalizations in science
can be interpreted as statements of uniform relationships between events or things in which temporally posterior occurrences
are posited as sufficient conditions. For example, the relationships between the governor on a steam engine and its regulated
speed, between the behavior of a guided missile and its target,
or between the flight performance of an automatically piloted
plane and its destination, can all be so expressed. As a matter of
fact, the whole new scientific field called cybernetics is devoted
to the study of this type of relationships. What is unproductive
is to translate such relationships into the framework of the more
orthodox cause-and-effect relationship and thereby to understand the phenomena of interest animistically by invoking "intentions," "purposes," "needs," etc.

It may be countered that since human behavior, unlike inanimate events, is after all purposive, or goal-directed, and since our intentions do affect our behavior, we must perforce use teleological explanations. To be sure, we do justify and understand our behavior, and that of others, in terms of these concepts, but scientifically they do not appear to have any more predictive power than such worn out concepts as instinct or free will. For one thing, not all human behavior has an objectively ascertainable purpose, nor does all purposive behavior produce intended results. It has proven difficult to establish regular connections between the "purpose," "goal," or "intention" on the one hand, and observable human behavior on the other, for it is practically impossible to determine the supposed motive factor conceived of in this manner. What a person reports as his intention or purpose may or may not be his "real" purpose or intention. In these post-Freudian days, we have learned to be suspicious of conscious introspections. Not only is it that man lies, which he undoubtedly does, but also that he sometimes does not know his own intentions. Except for our tendency to view events, nonhuman as well as human, animistically, "intentions" and "purposes" do not explain anything. Not yet, anyway.

5.

The content of this chapter can be briefly summarized. Functional explanation is teleological in that it postulates an as yet fully unrealized event, such as the maintenance of societal well-being, as the sufficient condition of the present or past social phenomenon. Scientific laws that rely on such principles of empirical regularity can be formulated, provided that the key terms are properly given determinately empirical significance. And such laws can be useful for explanatory and control purposes.

But functional analysis in sociology, of which the Davis-Moore explanation of social inequalities is a representative example, is characteristically vague about the end-state, or the goal, to which a given social phenomenon is supposed to be directed. Even more disconcerting is the situation that the supposed fact to be explained itself, namely social stratification, is inadequately defined as an observable and objective phenomenon, a circumstance that exposes the shaky empirical foundation of sociology fashioned in a grand style.

The appeal of functional analysis derives from the underlying teleology, which is shared by common sense. The views that things or events have a purpose and that they are caused by something are both part of common sense. When, however, the well functioning of a society is postulated as the purpose and cause of social inequalities, which is the crux of the Davis-Moore explanation, it has the logical consequence of making this phenomenon a necessary condition for the social end to which it is directed. This goes against an implicit tenet of functionalism that a goal can be attained via different routes, as well as offending the democratic ideal of equality to which most sociologists subscribe today. Despite these discomforts, however, functionalism lives, if not well, in current sociological thinking, because *intuitive understanding inherited from common sense has short-circuited tight reasoning and observation and has prevented empirical verification, or falsification, of functional explanations.*

VIII. Formalizing Common Sense

The prevalent mode of explanation in sociology today is subjective: conceived in terms of how a person perceives and interprets the situation he is in. Max Weber's sociology of understanding, a sample of which was analyzed in Chapter VI, is more than a prime example of this approach; it is one of the cornerstones of modern sociology. The subjective elements have been strong, if not as explicit, also in other sociologists who have contributed to the shaping of current sociological thinking. A survey of the present-day sociological literature reveals that the explanatory concepts which have gained favor among sociologists appeal to people's feelings, perception, awareness, beliefs, needs, outlook, etc., concepts which refer to the mental state, to use an old-fashioned phrase.

To name, briefly, a few better known examples: the notion of "relative deprivation," which is that a man's satisfaction depends not so much on what or how much he has as on how he perceives his relative advantage in comparison with relevant others ("reference groups"); the idea that under "cross pressure" a person desires and averts at the same time a course of action in about the same measure and consequently delays or avoids committing himself; the concept of "value-homophile," which is that people with similar beliefs make friends because they find each successive encounter gratifying and encouraging; the view that delinquency is a response to a "strain" resulting from the perceived discrepancy between a man's own expectations and those of others regarding his proper code of conduct; the notion that a man's behavior is affected by his awareness that his social status is unbalanced, for example, that his income is not in keeping with his education ("status inconsistency"); that feelings of congeniality ("cohesiveness") contribute to the productivity of a work team; that attitudes affect behavior. The underlying ideas are comfortingly familiar and plausible, though the labels may not be.

Attempts have been made to organize some of these frequently encountered explanatory principles into a system, a theory, that can operate deductively, as a scientific theory should. In such a system, as many as possible of these commonly accepted notions are subsumed under a handful of general principles, or postulates, which are stated explicitly as such. The process of deduction is also made more articulate, at least to the extent of justifying how a particular fact to be explained is related to one or more of the basic postulates, although no use may be made of formal logic or mathematics. These features in some recent sociological theories have been regarded by the more logically minded sociologists as signs that sociology is maturing as a science. There is no question that they reflect a break from the sociological tradition that mistakes verbal artistry or conceptual elaboration for scientific explanation. But the distinguishing mark of a scientific explanation is not its deductive structure, a rudimentary form of which is also discernible in nonscientific explanations, but its empirical verifiability. A deductive theory that pays no heed to this requirement of science, therefore, stops short of producing scientific explanations. After all, the Aristotelian pre-science of the Middle Ages was, if anything, thoroughly deductive.

1.

Two instances of sociological theories that are explicitly arranged in a deductive manner, starting with general propositions, will be discussed in this chapter. One is by George Homans, who states that all sociological explanations, insofar as they are explanations, are psychological in foundation and frankly admits that his theory draws on the explanatory principles ingrained in common sense. The principles are that social behavior, that is, interaction between at least two people, is an economic exchange based on reward and cost and that it is motivated by profit seeking. (Note the teleological overtone here.) He then translates some of the empirical generalizations of Skinnerian behavioral psychology in terms of reward and value, both of which are extrinsic to Skinner's basic scheme. It might be thought, as Homans apparently does, that he reduces social behavior to behavioral psychology, but what he does is really something else. He makes social behavior "understandable" in terms of these common sense notions via the Skinnerian principles of behavioral psychology. In a sense, he reduces even the latter to common sense and in the process obliterates the empirical aspects of the Skinnerian principles.

One of the basic propositions in Homans' theory, stated in his *Social Behavior: Its Elementary Forms,* is: "The more valuable to a man [call him *Person*] a unit of the activity another [call him *Other*] gives him, the more often he [*Person*] will emit activity rewarded by the activity of the other." Before going on with the analysis of how this proposition is used to explain observed events, it is useful to introduce some technical terms Homans employs. This can be done by referring to a basic experimental situation in Skinnerian behavioral psychology from which Homans borrows. When a pigeon pecks a disk placed in front of it (or simply raises its head above a certain measurable height), the psychologist feeds the pigeon some grain. When this "interaction" is repeated, it is observed that, following the psychologist's feeding, the pigeon's behavior of pecking (or head raising) becomes more frequent per unit time, or more probable in the technical sense of probability. Here the pigeon's behavior of pecking (or head raising) is called the "operant," the psychologist's behavior of feeding, "reinforcement," and the grain a "reinforcer." The process whereby the probability of the operant changes (i.e., increases) is called "operant conditioning," or simply "conditioning."

Now, Homans' proposition applied to a pigeon's behavior becomes: "The more valuable grain is to the pigeon the more often it will emit pecks that are reinforced with grain." But how is the value of grain to be determined, or measured, as Homans puts it? "When we say that at a particular time a pigeon values grain highly we refer to two sorts of fact. We mean, first, that grain reinforces the pigeon's behavior, that grain is a reinforcer or, as some sociologists say, *a value* to the pigeon, that our pigeon, if deprived of both grain and, say, thistledown for the same period of time, and now offered both, will eat the grain rather than the thistledown. And we mean, second, that the pigeon has recently gone without grain," that is, has been deprived of grain. To measure this second component of value, the psychologist "weighs the pigeon or counts the hours since it last fed. The value of the grain to the pigeon is greater, the thinner the poor thing is or the longer it has gone without food." Substituting this empirical definition of value in the proposition above, we have: If a unit of activity that *Other* gives *Person* is a reinforcer, the longer *Person* has been deprived of it, the more often *Person* will emit the activity rewarded by the activity of *Other*. Thus, as long as "value" is understood in the sense defined above, the concept does not add anything to Skinnerian psychology, though it may make the language somewhat simpler.

But the use of the term "value" tends to produce a detour around the empirical elements of the proposition and thus to remove the theory containing the proposition from empirical connections, rendering it untestable. The following analysis will show how this comes about. "The more *Person* needs help, the more often he will ask for it," is one of Homans' translations of his general proposition. Since, apparently what is needed is valuable, we may rephrase this principle as: If help is a reinforcer, the longer a person has been deprived of it, the more he will ask for it. In order to explain an activity as an operant, in general, then, it must be shown that it is accompanied by a thing, event, or another activity which is empirically established as a reinforcer and that this reinforcer has been deprived to some extent.

Homans uses this proposition to explain experimental findings from small group research, which may be briefly summarized as follows: Conformers communicate more with the nonconforming subject who holds views most removed from their own, while "deviates" (those who have independent opinions) communicate with others who hold views closer to theirs. (I will not go into how Homans defines "conformers" here; any common sense definition will do for the present purpose.) Of these conformers, Homans says: "Besides seeing a good chance of changing the opinion of a man who was alone in it, they may have found it more valuable to preach to the unconverted." (The other nonconforming subjects with whom the conformers could have communicated held views closer to themselves, though they were also alone.) But Homans' proposition cannot be said to explain these experimental results, unless it can be established empirically that "preaching to the unconverted" is a reinforcer for the conformers and that the conformers had been recently deprived of it, in comparison with "deviates," for whom this behavior is either not a reinforcer, or if it is, it had been withheld from them little or not at all. Homans does not show that any of these conditions held in fact in the experiment under consideration. Consequently, it looks as though Homans is assuming that "preaching to the unconverted" is valuable or is defining as valuable an activity that produces the supposed operant behavior in question. In the former, Homans would be invoking an ad hoc assumption, and in the latter, resorting to a tautology. By either route, any behavior that may be thought of as an operant can be "deduced" from the theory, that is, can be "explained." Under the circumstances, the theory is not falsifiable.

The foregoing is a typical example of how Homans fits data into his theory. Many a popular explanation that calls in concepts such as "needs," "want," "liking," etc., uses the same mechanism, as was pointed out in Chapter V. Saying that a

chain smoker smokes because he needs to smoke, or that Frenchmen drink wine because they like it, does not explain anything
since we infer the fact that the chain smoker needs to smoke
and Frenchmen like to drink wine from the behaviors that we
are supposed to explain.

As another example, take Homans' explanation of the following experimental findings: In an industrial investigation the researcher finds work groups that are "cohesive" have more
uniform production records in comparison with "uncohesive"
groups. The "cohesiveness" of a group is determined by the
workers' answers to the questions having to do with whether
they feel part of their work group, how they feel about moving
to another group, and how they feel their fellow workmen in
the group—in comparison with other groups—stick together, get
along with each other, and help each other. Approval is considered, both by Homans and Skinner, as a generalized reinforcer,
namely, one that is not innate or primary but serves the
function of many primary reinforcers—money, for example.
Homans interprets "cohesiveness" "measured" by the above
procedure as a sign of approval and the similarity in production
as an indicator that the workers are conforming to the production norms. He then takes the latter behavior as an operant that
is reinforced by "cohesiveness." (Homans also sees this as an
exchange in rewards, namely, approval and conformity, but this
aspect need not be considered here.) But what is the justification
for Homans' interpretation of cohesiveness as approval and similarity in production as a conforming behavior? Again, "cohesiveness" is considered a reinforcer here, because the similarity in
production is alleged to be an operant. The notion of approval
as a generalized reinforcer thus carries with it the danger of
degenerating into a dummy reinforcer which accommodates ad
hoc assumptions and produces circularities, unless its empirical
content can be made more determinate. Clearly, different kinds
of observable behavior can be fitted into "approval" for explanatory purposes by stretching here and squeezing there, but the
problem is acute if we wish to use the concept for verificational

purposes. These difficulties encountered in Homans' theory, despite its relatively sophisticated structure, arise from a less than rigorous use of concepts such as "value," "rewards," "approval."

2.

Together with the growing awareness that scientific explanation is deductive, there has been increasing interest in the formalization of theories in sociology. A formalized theory expresses the basic propositions and definitions in an abstract language, sometimes consisting of symbols; it is devoid of empirical content and uses a formal rule of reasoning, such as logic, in working out the relationships among the basic terms. This has the advantage of making the total structure of a theory visible at a glance, the assumptions explicit, and the terminology consistent within the theory. Formalization consequently makes it easier to detect circularities and ad hoc assumptions, if these should be resorted to in explanations. Mathematical physics is the most celebrated example of formalized theory, although the extent of formalization is by no means complete. Unlike geometry, which is a completely formalized system and does not depend on empirical correspondence for its validation, any empirical formal system must be accompanied by texts that describe the empirical things, events, or properties that the abstract terms stand for and specify what empirical relationships are expressed by the formal propositions, for example, mathematical equations. Without this linkage between abstract language and things of the senses, a formal theory is not a scientific one, and to the extent that the linkage is vague, it is difficult to relate the theory to facts, and hence to test it.

Formal theories have been attempted in sociology in recent years, including some with very difficult mathematical formulations, a development that is encouraging if for no other reason than to make the language of sociological discourse unambiguous and the line of reasoning clear. But so far these formal theories have paid less than serious attention to the empirical content of the theoretical terms, and their utility as scientific theories is more or less left in the air. The situation has been somewhat analogous to constructing an elaborate grammar in abstraction without paying much heed to the language in use to which it might be applied. In this respect, let us remember that mathematics in modern physics was first used in descriptions of empirical regularities and only thereafter in statements of physical laws involving abstract concepts; more systematic formalization of physics did not take place until the late nineteenth century. It is also sobering to remember that the medieval optics, which was mathematical, was sterile, because it was divorced from empirical observations.

An attempt to unify and formalize the more recurrent notions in sociological explanations has been made by James Davis in terms of a social-psychological theory called the "balance theory." It is perhaps not surprising to the reader by now that this theory puts the subjective view at the center of analysis. The balance theory is formal without being mathematical and displays some characteristic traits of a formal theory, although no formal system of deduction is used. In the way of imparting the flavor of a formal theory, I transcribe below the basic definitions and propositions of this theory, which is to be found in a recent volume by Berger, Zelditch, and Anderson, *Sociological Theories in Progress*, containing similar attempts at more formalized theories.

> The formal apparatus of the theory can be expressed in eight definitions:
>
> DEFINITION 1. A linear graph, or briefly, a *graph*, consists of a finite collection of *points, A, B, C, . . .*, together with all unordered pairs of distinct points. Each of these pairs (e.g., *AB*) is called a *line*.
> DEFINITION 2. Lines may vary in *type* (or "kind" of relationship) and *sign* (plus or minus) or *numerical value*.
> DEFINITION 3. The *net value* of a line of two or more types is the sum of the values for each type.
> DEFINITION 4. A *path* is a collection of lines of the form

AB, BC, . . . *DE,* where the points *A, B, C, D,* and *E* are distinct.

DEFINITION 5. A *cycle* consists of the above path together with the line *EA.*

DEFINITION 6. The *value* of a *cycle* is the product of the net values of its lines.

DEFINITION 7. A cycle with a positive value is *balanced,* a cycle with a negative value is *unbalanced.*

DEFINITION 8. The *net value of a graph* at point *P* is the sum of the values of the cycles in which *P* is a point.

It should also be noted that Definition 2 allows lines to vary in numerical value as well as sign. Consequently we will talk about the *value* of a cycle (assumed to be some number) as well as its *sign.*

So far, the apparatus presented is devoid of any content, and the definitions given could apply to people, switching circuits, messages, kinship relations, etc. . . . let us provide interpretations for points.

DEFINITION 9. *Person (P)* is the individual whose behavior is predicted by the theory, the point whose net value is being considered.

DEFINITION 10. *Other (O)* is some additional individual.

DEFINITION 11. *X* is some value or social object, sometimes a third individual.

Thus, in the analysis of voting, *P* might be a particular voter, *O* might be *Person's* best friend, and *X* might be a candidate or political party.

Our interpretations of lines are as follows:

DEFINITION 12. *Liking:*
This refers to a person's evaluation of something, as when *Person* likes or admires, approves, rejects, or condemns.

DEFINITION 13. *Unit formation:*
"In addition, there is a unit relation . . . the parts of such units are perceived as belonging together in a specially close way. But also two (or more) separate entities can form a unit. The two entities may be related through similarity, causality, ownership, or other unit-forming characteristics."

In order to shift from a language [namely, a collection of definitions] to a theory it is necessary to state the fundamental propositions or postulates from which the specific inferences or hypotheses of the theory will be drawn.

POSTULATE I: People prefer positive net values.
(a) If possible, people will act to shift the net value of their cycles from negative to positive or from a positive to a greater positive value.
(b) Low values are associated with feelings of distress, tension, discomfort, etc. The lower the value, the greater the distress (or dissonance).

POSTULATE II: Liking has a positive value; its opposite, disliking, has a negative value; indifference has a value of zero.

POSTULATE III: Unit formation has a positive value; its opposite, the segregation relationship, has a negative value.

The main proposition of the theory is stated in Postulate I (a), which is, incidentally, again teleological.

From this formal edifice, J. Davis obtains propositions of a general nature, which he calls "derivations." These derivations, if confirmed, would be empirical generalizations imbedded in a theory, or scientific laws. The first of these derivations is: "D1. The more similar *Person* is to *Other*, the more *Person* will like *Other*." Together with the definition of friends, "Definition 16. If P likes O and O likes P, P and O are friends," this derivation subsumes the notion of value-homophile, which, as will be remembered, means that people with similar values tend to make friends. A concrete instance of this principle is the empirical finding that among the people of Hilltown, a town in Pennsylvania with a fictitious name, those with similar attitudes toward blacks tend to be friends. The balance theory thus might be said to explain this fact.

But this derivation does not follow from the theory. In justification of the derivation, J. Davis argues as follows:

This proposition . . . is based on the following reasoning. We have considered P and O in terms of a set of attributes, one of which is X. The selection of X being arbitrary, each of the attributes can be an element in a balance cycle involving P and O. Now the more similar P and O are in terms of characteristics, the greater the proportion of the cycles with a positive $(PX)(OX)$ product. If, in turn, the $(PX)(OX)$ product is positive, a positive value for PO will raise the value of the cycle and thus add to net value. Because liking adds to the positive value of PO, it follows that similarity leads to liking.

Assume, then, that we have two pairs of persons, A and B, and C and D, and that there is a similarity in each pair, it being greater in the first than in the second. According to J. Davis' principle $(D1)$, the value of the product $(AX)(BX)$ is greater than the value of the product $(CX)(DX)$, both of which are positive. But there is nothing in the theory, including the above-quoted argument, which says that (AB) has to be greater than (CD). The theory simply says that under the conditions the values of (AB) and (CD) will both increase, but not that the value of (AB) will be greater than that of (CD), that is, that there will be more liking between A and B than between C and D. This is a problem of deductive logic which partly arises from not using a formalized calculus, such as symbolic logic or mathematics. Although this is not the focus of my criticism, it is interesting to note the lack of logical rigor in a theory with formal pretensions.

The reasonableness of the derivation $(D1)$ is in question on other grounds as well, grounds that are more apposite to my purpose. According to this derivation, we will have to conclude that there will be more liking between two middle-aged businessmen who are more similar to each other than a teenage boy and a teenage girl—say, Romeo and Juliet—who are less similar to each other in terms of diverse attributes, starting with sexual characteristics, family background, etc. Unless the words "similar" and "to like" are to be understood in a special but unspecified sense, this derivation does not look very promising as a generalization governing empirical observations. J. Davis rejects a subjective definition of similarity in terms of *Person's* perception, the vantage point from which the analysis is carried out in the balance theory, and defines it instead by the statistical measure of correlation coefficient.

> DEFINITION 14. Considering P and one or more *Others,* and a set of social attributes including X, the similarity between P and O *(symbolized by r_{PO})* is the correlation between P and O over all attributes other than X.

But a person possesses indefinitely many attributes, and hence unless some criteria are set up as to what attributes are to be considered relevant for the calculation of the correlation coefficient, similarity is empirically indeterminate. Certainly two persons who are similar in terms of biological attributes may not be so in terms of social ones. Besides, defining similarity objectively by the correlation coefficient has the consequence that similar persons like each other in equal measure, since similarity so defined is symmetrical: *Person* is similar to *Other* to the same degree as *Other* is to *Person*. This conclusion seems to contradict our experiences.

J. Davis stipulates that the principles embodied in the derivations are to be understood with the clause, "other things being equal." But unless these "other things" are specified, the theory is useless. To be sure, Boyle's Law does not always hold either, and it might be contended that the same *ceteris paribus* clause is invoked even in physical sciences. But in this case the conditions under which the law does not hold are known (namely, at high gas densities and low temperatures). And before these limitations were discovered, the law conformed to experimental data rather closely—closely enough to function as a basic empirical principle of chemistry.

This derivation *(D1)* might be said also to explain the experimental findings that the production rates are similar in cohesive work groups, which Homans explains by his theory. Cohesiveness, according to Homans is a kind of approval, and approval is an instance of liking, by J. Davis' definition; similarity in production among a group can, of course, be measured by suitably generalizing the correlation coefficient to handle more than two persons at the same time. Can we then expect (predict) that members of a cohesive group will also respect one another and admire one another, these behaviors being other instances of approval and liking? It is a *moot* question.

Thus, the balance theory again explains but does not predict and is immune to testing. The main reasons for this failure are that the theoretical terms cannot be related to empirical observations with any determinateness and that the theory relies on the escape clause of "other things being equal." (Incidentally, Homans also resorts to this stratagem.) J. Davis obtains many other derivations (fifty-six altogether) that explain, with varying degrees of plausibility, the better known notions in sociology, such as "cross-pressure," "relative deprivation," which undoubtedly attest to the theory's generality. But the balance theory is related to observations by weak links, and as long as these links remain weak it can not be tested.

3.

The two theories considered in this chapter represent a trend in sociology to construct explanations in a more deductive manner than has been the practice. In each case the structure of explanation is postulational, that is, explanations proceed from basic postulates (and definitions). One is more formal than the other, but without introducing mathematics or symbolic logic, a characteristic that has made it possible to examine features of a formal sociological theory without becoming too technical.

Both Homans and J. Davis render their theories plausible by fitting them over known facts and familiar conceptions. But this feat is accomplished by sometimes having to resort to circularities (especially Homans), convenient assumptions invented on the spur of the moment, or logical ellipses—all familiar tricks in everyday, loose thinking. These plus the stipulation that the explanatory principles are valid, in any event, only if some unspecified conditions hold, make it difficult to turn the theories upside-down, so to say, and to test the hypotheses that can be shown to follow unequivocably. Studies will undoubtedly have been made to test hypotheses which will be said to derive from these theories, but such tests would relate to the theories only tenuously and could not have any effects on them. If these theories persist, or are discredited, it will be more a matter of fashion than of empirical verification.

The concepts featured in these theories—"values," "approval," "similarity," "liking"—have familiar rings, and the connections among them can be grasped intuitively, vitiating empirical or logical rigor. It is this characteristic of the theories which makes explanations flow plausibly and which, at the same time, impedes the reverse process of verification. Thus the emphasis on the postulational and deductive structure of explanation and the attempts at formalization, both welcome developments in sociology, could merely promote a pseudo-science unless they are accompanied by other, more essential activities that make up science.

Measurement

Measurement occupies an important position in modern empirical sociology. Its basic meaning, however, has been misunderstood, and as a consequence current sociological practices related to measurement have tended to buttress and perpetuate the conceptual framework that needs to be overhauled before sociology can emerge as a science. This is the thesis to be developed in the remaining chapters, which include a critical examination of a typical measurement procedure and its methodological rationalization in sociology. The analysis is carried out in reference to fundamental notions of quantification and measurement and leads to a re-evaluation of the significance of measuring operations as related to concept formation in the beginning stages of sociology as a science.

IX. Quantification: The Empirical Basis

I T CAN BE said without exaggeration that the turning point in the development of modern science, what is referred to as the Scientific Revolution by historians, is characterized by a discernible replacement of qualitative concepts by quantitative ones. To cite more dramatic instances of this shift in the history of science: Galileo's experiments that were instrumental in abolishing the medieval notion of impetus and eventually led to what was to become Newton's law of inertia were predicated upon the quantitative concepts of distance and time. In chemistry, the development of which trailed behind that of physics, the turning point came with the abandonment of the theory of phlogiston when oxygen was discovered. The phlogiston theory persisted, roughly for a century, thanks to the inadequate attention paid to the changes in weight that substances undergo in chemical reactions. In establishing the identity of oxygen itself, weight was an important experimental variable which accounted for its characteristic reactions. The atomic theory, which dates back to the time of ancient Greece, did not become a viable scientific theory until the nineteenth century, and this was made possible by concentrating upon one property of the atom that is quantitative, namely, weight, to the exclusion of qualitative ones, such as color and shape. In the history of biology, which had been infused with the spirit of empiricism since the Renaissance, Harvey's discovery of the action of the heart marked a significant turn. In demonstrating the role of the heart as a pump, a simple and crude calculation of the volume of blood

111

that flows through the arteries spoke most eloquently to quiet the detractors.

The importance of quantification in science is generally recognized in modern sociology, and there is much preoccupation with making sociological concepts quantitative. It might be asked, then, what makes quantitative concepts so efficacious and so desirable? The reason seems to be twofold. First, quantitative concepts, in comparison with qualitative ones, make it possible to express relations among objects—things, persons, activities—in general and concise forms. For example, to indicate the relationship between religious affiliation and voting behavior, two qualitative concepts, it is not enough to say that they are related; it must be specified, for instance, that Catholics in comparison with Protestants are more likely to vote Democratic than Republican. In a country where there are more religious categories and political parties to contend with, statements of relationship between religious affiliation and voting, if any exist, would become very complex. In contrast, the simple statement that educational attainment is positively related to personal income implies a host of statements of the form: given two individuals, one with twelve years of schooling and the other with sixteen, the latter has a higher income than the former. Since there are many levels of educational attainment (measured in terms of years in school) and even more levels of annual income (measured in dollars), clearly this single statement embodies many potential statements about pairs of individuals and their incomes and educations. The fact that the general relationship between education and income stated above is only approximately true does not alter the logical character of the quantitative concepts. The second reason why quantitative concepts occupy such a central position in modern science is that they are peculiarly grounded in the shared observations of men, and provide strong links between theory and verification. These two aspects of quantification and its relationship to modern sociological practices will be examined in some detail in the following pages.

1.

Broadly speaking, objects in a set—observable entities, including persons and events as well as things—are said to be related
to one another quantitatively if it is meaningful to speak of one
being equal to or greater than another in some objective property in such a manner that the entire set can be ordered. The
property in which objects can be so compared and ordered is
said to be quantitative, a quantitative concept. Thus, a quantitative concept is relational. But it is not sufficient for a concept
to be quantitative that we speak of a thing being more or less
than another in some property. For example, just because we say
"I am holier than thou" it does not follow that holiness is quantitative in the same sense as warmth in the sentence, "The noon-
day sun is warmer in Italy than in Finland." The relationships
of equality and inequality must empirically satisfy certain conditions of order before a relational concept can be regarded as
a quantitative one.

The first of these conditions of order is that if a set of objects
is presumed to be quantitative, we must be able to say for any
two picked from this set whether one is greater than or equal to
the other. That is, *the objects must be connected* by the property in question. If, for example, we assume that there is a
hierarchy of social status in a small community, and hence think
of social status as a quantitative concept, the first test of this
supposition should be to see if we can say of any two families in
the community whether one is greater than or equal to the
other in social status. If we cannot make this comparison for a
significant proportion of the community for whatever reason,
the notion of social status as a quantitative concept has no empirical meaning.

Another criterion is *that the equality relationship must be transitive.* This means that if object A is judged to be equal in a
given property to B, and B in turn equal to C, then A must be
empirically judged to be equal to C. This may seem like a
self-evident criterion if we think of concepts that are known to

be quantitative, such as length, weight, and annual income in dollars. But it is not trivial for the purpose of deciding whether or not a concept is quantitative. For example, let us say that a gentleman, in comparing a brunette and a redhead, judges the brunette to be equal in beauty to the redhead, and the redhead to a blonde. But when he is confronted with the brunette and the blonde, the gentleman may definitely prefer the blonde, true to the cliché. If this should be the case, it must be concluded that beauty is not a quantitative concept as far as the three particular ladies and the gentleman are concerned, because the condition of transitivity for the relationship of equality is violated.

The condition of *transitivity also applies to the relationship of inequality.* That is, if A is judged to be greater in a given property than B, and B than C, then A must, in fact, be judged to be greater than C. This again may appear to be a truism in thinking about the number system, where this condition holds by definition. But many a would-be quantitative concept fails this requirement. To continue with the judgment of beauty, let us suppose that another gentleman prefers a redhead to a blonde, and the blonde to a brunette, but in comparing the redhead with the brunette, he finds that he does not prefer the redhead. Thus the relationship of "being more beautiful" is, in fact, not transitive, and the concept of beauty again cannot be regarded as a quantitative one in this very limited world of three beauties and a gentleman. This conclusion must be reached, it is to be noted, in spite of the fact that it "makes sense" for the gentleman to talk about a brunette being more beautiful than a redhead, etc., comparing two ladies at a time.

There are three other criteria of quantity that are logically as important as the above three but are less crucial empirically, at least in sociology, because they are less likely to stand in the way of a concept being regarded as a quantitative one. These three criteria may be stated briefly for the sake of completeness. One is that the equality relationship is symmetric (i.e., if A is equal to B, then B is equal to A); another is that the equality relationship is reflexive (i.e., A is equal to itself); and a third is that the inequality relationship is asymmetric (i.e., if A is greater than B, then it is not the case that B is greater than A).

In the foregoing, the relationships of equality and inequality ("being greater than," i.e., preference) were used in describing the conditions for the presence of a quantity, since these are familiar notions. But a collection of objects may be connected by any two relationships, one of which is symmetric, reflexive, and transitive, and the other asymmetric and transitive. It might just as well be said, in this case, that a quantity exists for the collection. That is, the six conditions given above are not only necessary but also sufficient for a quantity to be present. For example, given a heap of rocks, it is possible to pick two of them at a time and see if one scratches the other, or if one neither scratches nor is scratched by the other. The relationship of "scratching" is asymmetric and transitive, and the relationship of "neither scratching nor being scratched" is symmetric, reflexive, and transitive. That is, it can be demonstrated that if rock A scratches rock B, and B in turn scratches rock C, then A scratches C. If A neither scratches nor is scratched by B, then logically, B neither scratches nor is scratched by A. Empirically, if A neither scratches nor is scratched by B, and B neither scratches nor is scratched by C, then A neither scratches nor is scratched by C. And, of course, A neither scratches nor is scratched by itself. Thus the relationships concerning the behavior of rocks among themselves satisfy the conditions of quantity, although they are not expressions of equality and inequality, as we normally understand these terms. The operation of scratching one rock with another relates rocks quantitatively, and the associated relational concept may be given a convenient name, "hardness," for instance.

To give another example, in the army a corporal takes orders from a sergeant, a sergeant takes orders from a captain, but two corporals or two captains normally neither give nor take orders from each other. Here the relationship of "taking orders from" is asymmetric and transitive, and that of "neither taking orders from the other" is symmetric, reflexive, and transitive. This is as it should be, since a corporal, a sergeant, and a captain belong to a well-defined hierarchy of authority.

A quantitative concept, then, is one that relates objects in a series, like beads on a string, such that the progression in one direction in the series is accompanied by an increase in the magnitude of a property. Consequently, to say that object A has more of a quantity than B implies many other relationships, because this immediately indicates the relative position of A with respect to all other objects that have less of the quantity in question than B. In terms of the analogy of the string of beads, if we were to hold the string vertically and establish that bead A is above bead B, then we know, without being told so, that A is above all other beads that are below B.

We can also relate two quantitative concepts in succinct expressions, because a quantitative concept connects objects in this fashion. If we pair the elements in two series, we can say, for example, that as one series increases in magnitude, the other also increases, decreases, increases for a while then decreases, and so forth. That is, we can relate two concepts in a concise manner. The utter simplicity of such expressions might easily elude us, since we are so used to them. But perhaps we can appreciate the value of economy in expressions afforded by quantitative concepts by imagining a world in which there is no quantitative concept and everything is only related to everything else in terms of characteristics such as color, shape, taste, feel, etc.

2.

It is an empirical question involving human judgment whether rock A scratches rock B, and whether corporals take orders from sergeants. Empirically then what does it mean to say that rock A scratches rock B? First of all, it presupposes that a sharp edge of A is pressed against a flat surface of B and is drawn across it. Secondly, it signifies that this operation leaves a mark of indentation on the surface of *B*, which is discernible by observers of normal sensory faculties. Similarly, a corporal taking orders from a sergeant implies that the latter gives orders which the former executes. The behavior of the sergeant and the corporal must be observable and recognizable as constituting a chain of command and obedience. In each instance, then, there is an activity of relating an observable entity to another—drawing one rock against another, relating a corporal's action to a sergeant's orders. Secondly, the outcome of the operation is evaulated by a criterion or a set of criteria predicating human perception. These operations are required to ascertain empirically that a property satisfies the conditions of order for a set of objects. If an observer can verify, by these operations, that the conditions of order are satisfied for a heap of rocks, the rocks are quantitatively related as far as he is concerned. Similarly, of all the women he knows, if he can pick two at a time and can pronounce whether one of the two is more beautiful than the other or they are equally beautiful in such a manner that his pronouncements meet the conditions of order, beauty is a quantitative concept *for him* as far as his female acquaintances are concerned.

It is perhaps possible to define a quantitative concept in this individualistic sense, that is, by making the existence of a quantity dependent on the subjective criteria of a single person. By this procedure, what is a quantitative concept for an observer may not be quantitative for another. But concepts as we understand them are products of communal experiences. Especially in science, concepts serve as vehicles of communication, and for this reason a concept that is quantitative for some but not for others is useless for scientific purposes. Consequently, it must be stipulated that the criteria of quantity are to be established intersubjectively; that is, there must be an agreement among men about the operation of comparing one object with another and about the evaluation of such comparisons.

Again, the existence of such an agreement is an empirical question and often a matter of degree. It is our common experience that a man of normal sensory faculties can discriminate medium-sized objects, at least roughly, by hefting and can order them by the resulting sense data, provided that the objects are not too heavy, too light, or too close to one another in weight. There is also agreement among men about the way they order such objects by this procedure that is adequate for the practical purposes of everyday life. To be sure, objects of extreme size and weight cannot be ordered without the aid of an instrument; fine discriminations of weight also require an instrument. But the quantitative concept of weight does not derive from an instrument. Rather, the development of any weighing instrument depends on the concept of weight which is initially generated by the everyday practice of hefting common objects. With the use of an instrument the concept of weight becomes extended to cover very heavy (and also very light) objects and to detect minute differences among objects. But without the initial involvement of naked perception a quantitative concept does not arise to begin with. Indeed the use of an instrument itself requires naked perception and unison of sense judgments. An instrument merely aids the process of perception and agreement.

It is sometimes contended that a concept must precede any measurement; before a measurement can be made, that which is to be measured must be defined. This assertion holds if measurement is understood to mean instrumentation—development and use of instruments. But ordering objects—establishing the presence of a quantity—is an essential step in measuring (assigning numbers to objects by a rule that at least takes order into account), and in this fundamental sense the germ of a quantitative concept is to be found in measuring operations that are in everyday activities. There are quantitative concepts even in the physical sciences that are derived from other concepts and are calculated in terms of other directly measurable properties, e.g., density of matter, acceleration of a moving body, etc. But the basic quantitative concepts at the foundation of the physical sciences—length, weight, time—are formed from primitive operations of comparing objects and spontaneous agreement in comparative judgments satisfying conditions of order.

This point can be made more clearly in terms of concepts such as the pecking order of chickens or hardness of rocks, which cannot even be defined without referring to basic operations. The pecking order among chickens, for example, is determined by the relationship of a chicken pecking another, such that if chicken A pecks chicken B, but not vice versa, A is higher in the hierarchy of pecking order. By extension, a chicken that pecks all others is at the top of the hierarchy and the one that is pecked by every other without being able to peck any is at the bottom. The pecking behavior of chickens is an observable phenomenon about which there can be reasonably good agreement among observers. Furthermore, it apparently satisfies the conditions of order. The notion of pecking order clearly results from these empirical circumstances. It cannot be said that the behavior of chickens was invented to conform to the conceptual specification of pecking order. Similarly, it is not conceivable that the operations of measuring length, weight, and time were predicated by concepts that were handed down to us ready-made with no intervention of prior human experiences.

If motives were to be attributed to the initial, primitive operations of measurement they would have to be utilitarian in nature. And the successive refinements and eventual standardization in the measuring operations must be thought of as having been spurred on by the practical results brought about by such operations in science as in everyday affairs.

3.

In this context, the notion of social stratification in sociology can be thought of most conveniently as expressing an hypothesis of order among people. One of the things this concept signifies is that there is a hierarchy, an ordering, of people in terms of social status—prestige or honor that a man enjoys in his community. This is a commonly accepted principle in sociology.

The ordering is usually understood to be in terms of classes of people who share equal prestige or honor, and in this sense social status is allied to the idea of social class. To say that people can be ordered by social status is not different from saying that rocks can be ordered by hardness in formal terms. In each instance it means that entities can be compared with one another in such a way that human judgments of equality and difference among them satisfy the conditions of order. And in both cases human perception is involved, and the activities of comparison and evaluation are required. In the first instance, however, the entities concerned are people, while in the second they are rocks. But this is not a crucial difference, for there is nothing intrinsic about human beings which makes it impossible to detect objective differences or similarities among them. For example, we have little difficulty in discriminating people by height. What, however, does distinguish ordering people by social status from ordering rocks by hardness is that the criteria of comparison and evaluation are comparatively hazy where social status is concerned. It is relatively easy to specify what we have to do to see if one rock scratches another, but we do not know for certain what is to be done or what tangible things are to be looked at before we can decide if one person has a higher social status than another. This difference has to do with the operations underlying the ordering procedures, and it is a fundamental one bearing on the problems of sociology as an empirical science.

The idea that people can be ordered by social status is only an hypothesis, not a fact, because despite our vague feelings that there is a hierarchy of social status, it has not been demonstrated empirically that there is order with respect to this property. Methods have been devised for assigning numerical scores to people, presumably representing their social status positions, but these typically do not ascertain whether social status is a quantity (a consequence of which is that the numerical designations are only more or less arbitrary indicators of social status). These methods, which are sometimes referred to as reputational

methods, determine the social status position of a person by relying on the judgment of the community he lives in—a town or a
city, which for practical purposes means an aggregate of
judgments made by the "relevant" members of the community.
A typical reputational method—for example, the one August
Hollingshead used in his *Elmtown's Youth*—asks informed members of a community (sometimes referred to as judges, informants, or raters) to sort the names of the better known citizens
(sometimes called ratees), ranging from the reputable to the dis-
reputable, into classes of more or less equal social status,
defining this concept by a string of suggestive synonyms. If the
informants (judges) agree about who belongs in which class, it is
concluded that there is a genuine social status hierarchy in the
community. And then, depending on the interest of the investigator, he might go on to classify the rest of the community using
the ratees as the standards of classification. For example, a resident who is not one of the original ratees may be put in the
same class as those ratees with whom he shares relevant characteristics, such as income, education, residential neighborhood,
etc.

Our concern here is not so much with this last step, but with
the one at which it is decided that there is a hierarchy of social
status. The procedure described above relies on agreement
among the judges to the exclusion of other criteria of order.
Communal agreement is indeed a crucial condition for social
status hierarchy and, in a broad sense, for the existence of any
quantity. But the informants in the reputational method do not
comprise the entire community, and they usually do not even
constitute a representative sample. The same goes for the citizens
being judged, or the ratees. Under the circumstances, this
method at best shows that a social status hierarchy exists for the
socially visible. That is, the empirical condition of connectedness for order can only be shown to hold for the better known
and better informed citizenry. The secondary classificational
procedure whereby the more obscure are brought into the

supposedly hierarchical system does not contribute to the determination of that hierarchy and therefore does not change the state of uncertainty about the connectedness of social status.

The instructions given to the selected judges of social status, or informants, usually include an indication that the classes into which the ratees are to be sorted range from high to low, implying that these classes are ordered. This procedure, however, already assumes that the citizens themselves are ordered, and hence the conditions of order are in effect satisfied by fiat. For example, if an investigator stipulated that there are three social classes, "low," "middle," and "high," and if an informant places three citizens, A, B, and C, into the "low," "middle," and "high" classes, respectively, his judgments about the comparative social status of the citizens automatically satisfy the transitivity condition of inequality, because we immediately have the situation that C is higher than B, B is higher than A, and C is higher than A. It is essential to see that this result is obtained by the stipulation of the investigative procedure. In other words, the transitivity is imposed on the data rather than being discovered from them. If a judge is to place people into ordered classes, he could not violate the transitivity condition even if he wanted to, except by balking and infuriating the investigator. The situation is essentially the same even if the investigator does not specify the number of classes, as long as these classes are assumed to exist and to be ordered. The same logic applies to the other conditions of order as well.

But fundamental questions are beginning to be asked about the validity of the stratification hypothesis mentioned above and others related to it, and it is worth noting briefly two pieces of exploratory research recently carried out. The first makes use of Guttman scalogram analysis (described in a little more detail in Chapter XI), a method originally developed to measure attitude by ascertaining if verbal opinions about public issues or statements expressive of personal attitudes are ordered. Essentially, this method, by substituting people (citizens) for opinions and statements, makes it possible to decide whether the informants' judgments of other citizens (in comparison with themselves), with respect to social status, collectively satisfy the requirement of connectedness and, indirectly, the condition of transitivity of inequality. The requirement of connectedness, as it will be recalled, means that before a collection of entities— things or people—can be said to be ordered with respect to a property, it must be that any two from this collection can be compared with each other and a judgment can be made as to whether or not they are equal in the property in question.

This method was applied to a small New England community of between 500 and 600 families, from which a representative sample of about 50 nontransient residents were chosen and employed as both informants (raters) and citizens to be judged (ratees). The result shows that this community can be estimated to be connected by social status to about 9/10 of the optimum possible. It is a little difficult to report the conclusion concerning the transitivity condition in this space, because this condition was not directly tested but circuitously investigated through a technical device that cannot be described here. It is perhaps not incorrect to say that social status judgments can be thought to satisfy this condition only by causing another condition (asymmetry of inequality) to be violated to a significant extent. These findings are not such as to demolish the hypothesis of social status hierarchy, but at least they show that this hypothesis cannot be taken for granted. The 9/10 connectedness may seem a rather satisfactory figure, as far as this condition is concerned, but a reasonable projection would indicate that this figure will dwindle down to about 1/10 in a city roughly ten times the size of the particular community under consideration, one containing between 5,000 and 6,000 families. This would mean that an average resident of a community of moderate size could not make status judgments concerning the rest of the community except for about 10 per cent of it. Thus it must be concluded that from the point of view of the connectedness criterion alone the concept of social stratification tied to people's perception of other people's status presents a serious difficulty anywhere but in very small communities.

The other piece of research attacks a slightly different hypothesis of social stratification, that of occupational prestige. This hypothesis says that different occupations carry different amounts of prestige or honor. This too has long been more or less taken for granted, and it is only recently that empirical findings have tended to show that prestige judgments about occupations may violate one or more conditions of order, especially the transitivity of inequality. The research under consideration questions whether a person can consistently order a set of relevant occupations by prestige, and if so, whether people agree in their ordering. If both queries are answered in the affirmative, it may be concluded that occupational stratification by prestige is an objective reality. But if the answer is affirmative just to the first question, occupational stratification must be said to have subjective significance only.

In the present research, a fairly homogeneous collection of about a thousand university students were asked to compare twenty-one occupations, ranging from physician to soda fountain clerk, two at a time. The object was to find out whether, for each student, the conditions of order are satisfied to produce a hierarchy, and, if so, whether there is agreement among the individual hierarchies. The findings indicate that the students as individuals have no trouble ordering the occupations, but that there is only middling agreement among them. One meaning of the result from this exploratory research may be that social stratification, at least in terms of occupational prestige, is a mental picture that people carry around, rather like our image of the sun rising and setting everyday, but it may not be an objective (intersubjective) reality. In other words, we may be able to pigeonhole our friends and enemies, for example, by their occupations, into individual categories of more or less prestige, but these may not add up to defining an objective system of classes that has the same meaning for everybody.

These studies, especially the second one, are only preliminary to more extensive investigations that must be carried out in this area, and the conclusions must be taken with caution. But they do indicate how what is regarded as a quantitative concept, such as social status, cannot be taken at its face value. Treating such a concept as if it were quantitative and giving it numerical expressions (for example, social status index numbers) does not make it a quantitative concept. To quantify does not simply mean numerical representation of differences among objects in a property. In order to do this, the objects must be related to one another with respect to the property of interest in the manner discussed in the first two parts of this chapter. Quantification signifies making use of concepts denoting such properties in explanatory schemes. If, therefore, sociology is to become quantitative, it must look for and build upon concepts that have a quantitative basis in everyday practices, instead of putting a quantitative facade on nonquantitative concepts of common sense appeal. Not all concepts that can be shown to be quantitative in the sense discussed here will have equal sociological import. Which quantitative concepts will be most useful in the end can only be judged by the results they produce in the context of scientific explanation. In this light, *the fundamental quantitative concepts of sociology have not yet been discovered.*

X. Measurement and Mathematical Expressions

MEASUREMENT in a strict sense is the representation of a quantitative concept by another that acts as a standard because of its well-known properties. This standard quantity is, of course, the system of numbers, which can be thought of as a set of ordered objects identified by numerals. (The relationship between numbers and numerals is the same as that between things and their names. Thus a number can be represented by different numerals, e.g., Arabic, Roman, Chinese, etc., just as common objects are given different names in English, Swahili, Chinese, etc.) The relationships among the numbers are so well known that if we can link numbers with objects by some nonarbitrary procedure, we can surmise the relations among the objects by examining the numbers representing them. This is the logic of measurement. An advantage of numbers in this role is that they can represent an infinite number of things and with infinitesimal gradations. Their added attraction, as far as science is concerned, is that they make mathematics, a highly systemized tool of reasoning, available for working out relationships among the things to be explained.

In a broader sense, measurement may not involve a quantity. But in this case the use of numbers all but loses its significance, and much of mathematics, which was instrumental in the development of modern science, is inapplicable. For this reason, I choose a narrower definition of measurement for the present purpose, which is to discuss mathematical expressions in sociology in relation to quantification and measurement.

In measurement, the linkage between objects and numbers is governed by a known rule, or we cannot fathom from the numbers anything about the relationships among the objects they represent. Numerical representation of things is, in the final analysis, drawing an analogy between numbers and things, and the parallel between the two, as with any analogy, is more complete in some instances than others. In likening a set of objects to numbers, then, we must be aware of how far we intend or are able to draw on the numerical analogy, for, to the extent that the numerical analogy is not complete, only a limited range of mathematics can be used in relating the measured concepts. If limitations imposed by measurement are not heeded, numerical representation and manipulation can easily turn into mysticism, as has happened on occasion since the time of Pythagoras, and it is well to ponder the *limitations* inherent in the numerical symbolization of objects.

1.

Limitations that measurement places upon mathematics can be discussed by introducing the notion of scales and permissible transformations. Depending on how close or remote an analogy we wish to draw between numbers and objects, we obtain different scales of numbers. Three principal scales are customarily discussed: ordinal, interval, and ratio scales. Numbers that represent order among objects make up an ordinal scale. For example, numbered slips given out to customers at some bakeries denote the order in which the customers are to be served and can be thought of as forming an ordinal scale. When objects are represented by numbers, such that these indicate not only the order among the objects but also the relative distances or intervals among them, the numbers are said to form an interval scale. Calendar time, for instance, measures time by an interval scale. Thus, the birth years of the children in a given family tell not only the order in which they are born, but also the time intervals separating them. Temperature measured by an ordinary thermometer is another example of interval measurement. Lastly, numbers that reflect the proportionality among the objects that they represent constitute ratio scales. Weight in pounds and annual income in dollars form ratio scales. An income of $20,000 a year is twice as much as $10,000 a year, just as a man weighing 200 pounds is twice as heavy as a boy weighing 100 pounds. Numbers in a ratio scale, of course, impart information about order and intervals as well. Ordinal, interval, and ratio scales can thus be thought of as containing successively more information about the objects being measured.

The three scales can also be characterized in terms of the kind of transformation one can perform on the numbers, and this approach brings out the mathematical limitations inherent in each. If we are interested in changing the numbers in an ordinal scale, we have to take care that the numbers represent the same order before and after the transformation; within this limitation, however, an ordinal scale may be transformed to another quite freely. For example, five customers holding slips marked 11, 12, 14, 15, and 16 can turn their slips in for others marked 20, 30, 40, 50, and 60, respectively, and they would be served exactly in the same order as before. This kind of order-preserving change of numbers is called monotone increasing transformation. The range of changes we can make on interval numbers is more limited. If we are to transform the numbers in an interval scale, the resulting numbers must also form an interval scale such that all the information contained in the initial scale is preserved. This condition is satisfied if the transformation is of the form $X' = aX + b$, where X and X', respectively, represent numbers before and after transformation, a is any positive number, and b any real number. This is a general linear equation and the transformation it produces is referred to as linear transformation. For example, temperature measured in centigrade degrees (C) can be transformed to Fahrenheit degrees (F) by the equation $F = 9/5 C + 32$. And, lastly, the equation that correctly transforms a ratio scale into another takes the form $X' = aX$, where X and X' represent scale values and a, any positive number, as before. This is known as similarity transformation. Thus, weight in pounds (P) can be transformed to grams (G) by the equation $G = 453.6P$ without losing any information. Similarity transformation is the only kind that preserves the ratio relationships among the objects measured.

It is evident that there is a direct relationship between the amount of information a scale imparts and the restrictiveness of transformation permitted. The ratio scale, which is the most informative of the scales being considered, is most restricted in the admissible transformations. At the other extreme, ordinal scales, which contain the least amount of information, allow monotone increasing transformations, which means that the other two transformations may also be performed without distorting the information. It can be shown that the arithmetic operations of addition and subtraction are meaningless on scale values that permit monotone increasing transformations, i.e., ordinal numbers. That is, no useful information can be obtained by adding or subtracting two numbers that represent ordinal values. One consequence of this is that we cannot calculate the most frequently used statistical measures of a variable that can be measured only ordinally; these measures are conceptually meaningless where ordinal data are concerned. For example, the calculation of the average, called the arithmetic mean in statistics, entails adding up a set of numbers and dividing the sum by the number of cases involved. Consequently, this measure cannot be calculated for ordinal numbers such as those marking bakery tickets. An average calculated on such numbers would tell us nothing. The same is true of other, more complicated statistical concepts. There are special statistical techniques intended for ordinal numbers, especially those representing ranks, although these are limited in number and in what they do as statistical tools. But this circumstance in no way changes the fact that the range of permissible mathematics is delimited by the measurement procedure used.

It is also useless to make ratio comparisons among ordinal numbers. For example, of the six runners in a race who come in first, second, third, etc., it would be obviously wrong to conclude that the third arrival is three times as slow as the first, or that the sixth is twice as slow as the third. Such comparisons are

equally inappropriate for interval numbers. For example, it
would be absurd to say that a pan of water registering 10°C. is
twice as warm as another measuring 5°C. The unreasonableness
of this statement can be seen by transforming these readings to
the Fahrenheit degrees, i.e., 50°F. and 41°F., respectively,
which clearly do not stand in the 2-to-1 ratio. Similarly, the Intelligent Quotient is measured in an interval scale, and it would
be erroneous to regard a man with an I.Q. of 140 as being twice
as "intelligent" as another with 70. To give another example,
the National Opinion Research Center has calculated the prestige scores for 90 more or less commonly known occupations for
the purpose of rank ordering them by prestige. These scores,
ranging between 33 (shoe shiner) and 96 (supreme court justice),
clearly do not form a ratio scale, and it would make no sense to
say that the mail carrier with a score of 66 is twice as prestigious as the shoe shiner who is given the score of 33.

But it is quite proper to compare, in terms of ratio,
differences between pairs of interval numbers, that is between
intervals; all arithmetic operations are of course also applicable
to them. Thus it is correct to say that the interval between the
first born of a family (seven years old) and the second born
(three years old) is twice the interval between the second and
the third born (one year old). Similarly it is perhaps unexcep-
tionable to interpret an increment of 10 points in the I.Q. over a
generation among, say, blacks in an integrated community, as
being twice as much as a growth of 5 points in another population. It is less obvious, however, if the occupational prestige
scores can be treated in the same manner, since it is uncertain
that these scores form an interval scale. Sums of interval
numbers can also be compared to each other, though not in the
ratio sense; differences among such sums are meaningful and can
be subjected to usual arithmetic operations. For these reasons,
most statistical techniques are available for variables measured
or measurable in interval scales.

All the mathematical operations permissible on interval
numbers are, of course, quite appropriate for numbers deriving

from ratio scales. Moreover, ratio comparisons are obviously also possible among these numbers, since they represent ratio relationships among the objects they designate. But only ratio scales allow such comparisons, and mathematical statements involving ratios are properly reserved for variables that can be measured in, or at least conceptualized as, ratio scales.

2.

The question of how objects are represented by numbers, that is, by what kind of scale, is an empirical question having to do with the actual measurement procedure, and cannot be decided a priori. A concept that is measurable now only by means of an interval scale may be modified to be measurable in a ratio scale in the future, as happened in the case of temperature, which can now be measured in absolute degrees (Kelvin). But such a development itself depends on the discovery of empirical laws that make measurement procedures possible and meaningful. Where such an empirical basis is lacking, treating a concept as though it were measurable in ratio scale could have misleading consequences if taken seriously. This point can be illustrated with an example from sociology.

The following equation, formulated by George Homans, is supposed to show the relationship between satisfaction and reward attendant upon an activity: $S = aR/(Q-R)$. In this equation, S stands for satisfaction derived from an activity, R for the total amount of reward received from the activity, and Q for the amount of total reward at the satiation point. $(Q-R)$ would therefore mean the amount of reward wanting from the point of complete satisfaction, while a is a constant of proportionality and is of no particular importance for the general shape of the relationship. This equation then says that satisfaction is proportional to the total amount of reward received and inversely proportional to the amount of reward falling short of the satiation point. By making a couple of assumptions concerning the frequency of activity (F_A) and the frequency with which this activity is rewarded (F_R), which need not be explicitly stated here, it can be shown that the satisfaction and the frequency of activity, which might be equated to productivity in certain situations, vary together; that is, $F_A = S$, if and only if the following condition holds:

$$F_R = aR/b(Q-R)^2,$$

where b is another constant of proportionality.

Now, this is an elegant looking formula, but *as a statement dealing with observable phenomena it is meaningless*. It would make sense only if we assume that the key terms in the equation are measurable in ratio scales because of the mathematical relationship involved. In particular, we would have to assume that reward as well as satisfaction are concepts that admit of ratio comparisons. Granting these assumptions, then, the equations $S = aR/(Q-R)$ and $F_A = S$ together imply that both the satisfaction and the frequency of an activity, or productivity, increase as the total reward received. Moreover, as the reward approaches the point of complete satisfaction, the satisfaction and productivity accelerate until they reach enormous proportions, approaching infinity. It is perhaps conceivable that such a state of satisfaction exists, but it is difficult to think of a productivity that is measured in the same units as satisfaction and approaches infinity. Furthermore, the condition $F_R = aR/b(Q-R)^2$ implies that, in order to keep the productivity in pace with the satisfaction as the reward grows, the frequency of reward will have to be increased even more rapidly than both satisfaction and productivity. Again, it is difficult to give empirical meaning to such expressions. What does it mean to reward an activity with a certain frequency, let alone with a frequency approaching infinity? Homans gives a hypothetical interpretation: "Suppose, for instance, that soldiers have been fighting a battle all day, and at dusk the enemy is just beginning to give way [$(Q-R)$ decreases]. Then they will put on a last big push [enormous F_A], and their elation [S] will mount rapidly as they get sight of victory." Is getting sight of victory to be understood to mean high frequency of reward? It may indeed be a large reward, but it seems arbitrary to equate it with frequency of reward.

It may be argued that it is not the business of a theorist to worry about how his concepts may be given empirical meaning so that the theory may be verified, and that it is rather the task of experimentalists to devise suitable measurements for the concepts according to the theoretical specifications. If the equation involving the concept of satisfaction presupposes that satisfaction is to be measured in a ratio scale, a theorist might say, "Then invent a measurement technique that will give us ratio measurements of satisfaction." This may be an acceptable argument in highly developed and formalized sciences such as physics and chemistry, but in sociology, where empirical generalizations of a descriptive nature are yet to be formulated in unambiguous terms, it is fruitless to postulate theories in terms of concepts that cannot be empirically interpreted in the sense dictated by the theory. The point is not that terms like satisfaction and reward have no empirical meaning. Quite the contrary; they are taken from the everyday language and, if anything, have *too much* common sense meaning attached to them. It is rather that there is no empirical basis for the meaning attributed to them by the mathematical equations.

To draw a parallel, it used to be quite common to speak of sins that weigh on one's conscience. On the strength of such an expression, a theorist might proceed to formulate mathematical equations relating the weight of sins to the elevation of the soul. And experimentalists might be charged to come up with measures of these concepts. (Recently a rich man in the United States offered a large sum of money to anyone who would empirically prove the existence of the soul, preferably by photographing it.) We would most certainly reject such a procedure, and the reason is not that we cannot ever proceed from theory to observation, but rather that any measure of sin's weight that we might invent is arbitrary because there is no accepted practice of measuring the entity. Sociological concepts such as "satisfaction" and "reward" are not as démodé with us as "sin" or the "soul"; but it seems unwarranted and misleading to use them in mathematical expressions implying ratio relationships. Such a practice tends to create a false impression that the sociological concepts so used are measured, in the sense defined in this chapter, when, in fact, they may not even have the empirical basis to be considered quantitative. This misconception, together with the postulational and formal approaches to theory-building, helps foster the scientific appearance of sociology and at the same time delays the development of truly meaningful sociological measurements.

XI. Anomie:
"Measuring" the Unmeasurable

O NE OF the vexing problems in sociology today is thought to be how to *measure* important sociological concepts so that theories couched in them could be given empirical substantiation. The more empirically minded of modern sociologists, accordingly, strive to measure what they conceptualize, often even when it defies measurement. Indeed, it would appear that to a modern sociologist there is no concept which in principle cannot be measured. A result of this approach is a proliferation of scores, scales, indicators, and indices. A concept is sometimes "measured" by different procedures often leading to results that do not agree. Under the circumstances, a question naturally arises as to whether these numerical procedures measure what they are really supposed to measure, that is, whether they are "valid," and much effort is expended in answering this seemingly reasonable question. But this is really a wrong question to ask, since it is generated by the false premise that concepts born of speculation have determinate significance and can always be measured.

1.

To proceed with an example, there is a widespread notion that alienation is responsible for disturbing social events (which we call social disorders) such as rioting, looting, and murder. This notion is shared by both the general public and sociologists, who in no small measure contribute to this view. When Robert Kennedy was shot, a radio commentator remarked that the attacker was an alienated person, even before his identity was known, with the implication that alienation was responsible for the shooting. This bit of theorizing may "explain" the assassin's behavior to the man in the street and make him "understand" the perplexing event. The word "alienation" here acts as a label, and often the act of labeling passes for explanation. In other ages and other places, labels such as original sin, evil spirits, God's will, and fate played the same role. This sort of explanation by labeling invariably involves a circularity, and it was shown in the preceding section how typical sociological theories manifest the same characteristic.

It is tautological to say that the assassin shot Kennedy because he was alienated and to establish his state of alienation by his act of assassination. This circularity could be broken by showing that the assassin was indeed alienated before and up to the moment of shooting, or by a criterion independent of this act. It is, of course, not necessary in this case that alienation be *measured* in the sense defined in the preceding chapter; an objective judgment of whether or not a person is alienated is all that is called for. But typically in today's sociology this need for an objective and noncircular description is construed in terms of *measurement*.

Given the concept of alienation and the explanation it affords, the more empirically minded sociologists would proceed to measure this concept to show that the explanation is a noncircular and viable one. In this endeavor sociologists encounter the difficult question of validity of measurement, that is, whether or not the measurement really measures alienation. But the problem is really one for which there is no satisfactory solution, because, first, the word "alienation" has no determinate meaning such that one can say unequivocally of another that he is or is not alienated, and, second, there is no apparent agreement in the way the word is understood by different people. It is possible to make the meaning of alienation arbitrarily determinate by deciding to call a person alienated if he manifests such and such characteristics and by sanctifying this decision with the testimonial approval of other sociologists. By this method, the concept of alienation can be saved from the fate of circularity and given empirical substantiation if the alienated people thus defined should contain among them a greater proportion of assassins and criminals of other types than their nonalienated counterparts. But if this should in fact not be the case, a doubt would linger that the "measurement" of alienation lacks validity, and the fate of our favorite explanation would hang in mid-air. Even if the alienation hypothesis should be confirmed with the employment of the particular "measurement," the only sure thing that could be said would be that we have discovered a criterion which discriminates assassins and other types of criminals from less disturbing people. It would not settle the question whether or not this criterion is coterminous with alienation as generally understood.

2.

To give this discussion a sharper focus, let us consider "anomie," a term closely related to "alienation," which nevertheless has had a narrower sociological usage than "alienation" and has left a discernible trace of theorizing and research. "Anomie" connotes something similar to "alienation" and has sometimes been used interchangeably with it. Its usage, however, has been more among sociologists than the general public, and the concept has been given less diverse verbal definitions. It was introduced into sociology by Emile Durkheim, one of the first modern sociologists, and was picked up again more recently by the most frequently cited sociologist of the contemporary scene, Robert Merton. It has been subjected to the most sophisticated measurement techniques open to sociologists, not just once but several times, with technical success nearly every time, and has been used often to test hypotheses involving the notion of anomie. A critical review of the progress and problems of this concept in contemporary sociology would therefore admirably illustrate how mainstream sociology has been brought to an impasse by the emphasis on measurement.

Anomie, as conceived by Durkheim, refers to a situation in which the individual is loosened from socially induced restraints on his "appetites," "desires," "aspirations," and "passions." Durkheim thinks that some form of restraint on these forces is desirable for the psychic well-being of a person, for when all restraints are removed, human aspirations swell up to infinite proportions while the means for reaching these goals remain constant, or at any rate, fall far short of the soaring goals. The consequence of anomie, therefore, is perpetual frustration and disillusionment.

Durkheim identified two different forms of anomie, economic and marital, corresponding, respectively, to a removal of regulations on material and sexual appetites. Economic anomie results in times of economic crisis *and* prosperity when the forces regulating economic propriety are weakened, and it exists more or less chronically in the commercial and industrial sector of modern capitalist society, which is committed to unceasing acquisition and accumulation. Marriage, especially monogamy, regulates and channels sexual drives, Durkheim believes, and when marital obligations are missing, as among bachelors or among divorced or widowed men, sexual appetite spirals without being satiated, and sexual anomie obtains. (Durkheim contends that women are naturally more restrained sexually and the lack of marital regulations does not have the same effect on them.) Anomie, in sum, is the state of de-regulation of desires, and its consequences are "despair," "disillusionment," and "unhappiness."

Merton, who claims to follow in the footsteps of Durkheim, has a more general view of anomie. To him anomie exists when commonly accepted goals cannot be reached because legitimate means of attaining them are inaccessible. This could happen, presumably, when the goals are set too high, as in Durkheim's conception, or when social forces withhold from certain classes of people the means that are open to others, as Merton maintains. The effect of this disparity between goals and means is said to be normlessness, which might be interpreted as more-than-incidental disregard for norms and confusion about them in the society. Where Durkheim was almost exclusively concerned with de-regulation of goals, Merton puts more emphasis on dissolution of norms circumscribing the means which results in various types of social deviance. Merton suggests that the psychological effect of the anomic state is "uneasiness" and "sense of isolation," and in extreme cases, "anxiety." Merton thinks of this effect of anomie as the psychological component of anomie, as opposed to the sociological, which is the state of normlessness. Recent sociological discussions about anomie, characteristically enough, have been almost exclusively centered around the psychological aspect. It is to be noted that to Durkheim the psychological correlate is "disillusionment," "despair," and "unhappiness," while it is "uneasiness," a "sense of separation from the group (isolation)," and "anxiety" for Merton. Do these two sets of words refer to the same thing? This question could be answered in a meaningful manner if the terms involved had determinate denotations, but unfortunately the words are more suggestive than denotative, and any attempt to answer the question would degenerate into a verbal disquisition.

It has been proposed, by the sociologist Leo Srole, that the psychological effect of anomie on a person, his "anomia" (Srole's word) be measured by how he reacts to the following statements:

1. Most public officials are not really interested in the problems of the average man.
2. These days a person doesn't really know whom he can trust.
3. Nowadays a person has to live pretty much for today and let tomorrow take care of itself.
4. In spite of what people say, the lot of the average man is getting worse, not better.
5. It's hardly fair to bring a child into the world with the way things look for the future.

A man who endorses all these statements is supposed to be the most anomic, and one who does not endorse any, the least; in general, the more statements one endorses, the more anomic he is. This claim is made on the basis of how people's reactions to these statements are related to one another rather than on any concrete evidence that they faithfully render the state of anomie. It is perhaps worthwhile to explain briefly this technical point here since it is often confused with the question of validity.

Research experience has shown that the responses to the above statements display the same characteristics as responses to the statements of the following form:

1. I am at least 5 feet feet tall.
2. I am at least 5 feet 6 inches tall.
3. I am at least 6 feet tall.

Now if we imagine four persons whose heights are 6 feet 2 inches, 5 feet 7 inches, 5 feet 2 inches, and 4 feet 11 inches, it is clear that the first, the tallest, person must endorse all three statements, the second the first two statements, the third just one statement, and, the last, the shortest, none of the statements. Obviously, we can order the individuals, though only crudely, by the number of statements that they endorse. This is possible because the statements are related to the continuum of height in such a way that the position of a person on the continuum determines the number *and* the identity of the statements he has to endorse. For example, a person who is 5 feet 7 inches tall has to endorse two statements and these have to be the first two. Conversely, if a person is to endorse two statements, these have to be the first two; he could not very well endorse statements 1 and 3 but not 2, or 2 and 3 but not 1, without being inconsistent. Thus we could order individuals by the number of statements that they endorse, and the result would be a correct, though rough, ordinal classification by height.

A set of statements in which there is this kind of determinate relationship between the number and identities of the statements that one endorses is thought of as defining a continuum and is said to form a *Guttman scale*, after Louis Guttman, who invented this technique of measurement. The Guttman technique of scaling has been most extensively used in measuring attitudes, and experience in this field of investigation has shown that it is not easy to construct statements expressing different degrees of an attitude that scale in the technical sense defined above.

Srole has shown that his statements form a Guttman scale on a sizable number of people, and others have since repeated the demonstration on other groups of people. Moreover, Srole's statements have been shown to define a continuum of a psychological state by other criteria of scaling than Guttman's. Thus, at least on technical grounds, it must be admitted that Srole's statements seem to be a reliable tool for measuring something about the disposition of human beings. But the question is, "What?"

A characteristic of the Guttman technique of scaling, shared by other methods of measurement, is that it does not tell us what the scale that it produces measures. What it measures, that is, what it means in the substantive context of a science, can only be determined *empirically*. And the question of whether a scale, say Srole's scale, really measures what it is supposed to, that is, anomie, or at least its psychological component, is an empirical question, and it is pointless to ask it if no empirical operations are available that might provide the answer. Let us see how we might decide whether Srole's scale measures anomie. Following Srole's usage, this scale will henceforth be referred to as "anomia," whenever it is convenient, to distinguish it from anomie, which it is supposed to measure.

4.

On the face of it, it is not apparent that a person who endorses all five of Srole's statements, supposedly one who is as anomic as can be measured by this instrument, is more anomic in the psychological sense than another who endorses fewer of the statements. That is, it is not evident that the former, in comparison with the latter, possesses more of the anomic characteristics given either by Durkheim ("disillusionment," "despair," "unhappiness") or by Merton ("uneasiness," "sense of isolation," "anxiety").

If we had an objective way of judging a person to be more disillusioned, more in despair, etc., than another, so that we could say that the degree of disillusionment, despair, etc., is positively related to Srole's scale scores, it might be possible to directly validate this scale of anomie. To revert to the three statements concerning height for illustration, they form a scale supposedly measuring height, which produces four classes of people by height, each with a score varying between 0 and 3, the numerals representing the number of statements endorsed. In this instance, it can be shown directly that persons who receive the score of 3, for instance, are taller than those with a score of 2, 1, or 0; those with a score of 2 are taller than others with a score of 1 or 0, and so forth, by actually comparing two persons at a time, back to back. There are, of course, easier and more refined methods of measuring height, so that we would not normally want to measure height by the Guttman technique. But, the point is, even if better methods were not available so that we would have to rely on Guttman scaling, we could validate the Guttman scale by a direct comparison of persons in terms of height. In the case of anomie, such a procedure is not available to us, and Srole's scale of anomie cannot be directly validated. Can it be *indirectly* validated?

The concept of anomie has figured prominently in modern sociology and has led to hypotheses of a behavioral nature. To Durkheim, anomie is a cause of suicide, because, in his words, "How could the desire to live not be weakened under such anomic conditions?" On the other hand, anomie results from certain objective conditions: in times of economic prosperity, when wealth is acquired suddenly, which further whets the appetite for more; in times of economic disaster in which men of wealth are drastically brought down to the common level without being able to adjust their life goals to their reduced means; among business men whose creed is greed; and, among single, widowed, and divorced men for whom sexual appetites are unbridled relative to married men and to women in general.

First of all, we should expect suicides to receive high anomia scores. But we cannot very well measure the dead by Srole's method. It should also be the case, however, that the incidence of suicide is high among those who measure highly anomic by Srole's scale, if this really measures anomie. To verify this expectation empirically, it would be necessary, at the least, to measure the anomic state of a million or so persons, say in the United States, and wait around for the lifetime of these people to determine which ones commit suicide in the end. The anomic scores of the suicides can then be compared with those of the nonsuicides. This large number is needed for the investigation because, assuming that the suicide rate is about 100 in 1,000,000, we could expect to have scores for about 100 eventual suicides for comparative purposes. Admittedly it is difficult to carry out such an investigation; it would be time consuming and costly, not to speak of the more technical problems of keeping track of the people being studied, ascertaining the cause of death, controlling for extraneous factors, etc. Be that as it may, such research has not been reported, to my knowledge, and we have no evidence that anomie as measured by Srole's scale leads to suicide.

The supposed relationship between anomie and its antecedents, for example economic prosperity or martial status, are of course easier to investigate, and there is more empirical evidence bearing on the measure of anomie taken from this point of view. To begin with, apparently, there is some indication that men who are single, widowed, or divorced tend to receive larger scores on the Srole scale than married men. I am not aware of studies that directly show the effect of disasters such as demotion, loss of a job, or bankruptcy on the anomia reading of the victims. Recent findings, however, seem to suggest that anomia is higher among persons displaced by endemic banditry in comparison with similar but nondisplaced persons. It is, of course, debatable as to whether displacement due to a calamity of this nature can be equated to what Durkheim had in mind in speaking of economic disasters, but its effects on normlessness and its psychological concomitants might not be too different.

Durkheim's views concerning sudden economic prosperity might be interpreted to mean that persons who better their positions socially and economically relative to their origins—those whom sociologists call upwardly mobile—would be subjected to anomic influences for the following reason. Upward social mobility means breaking through the class barrier, say between the blue-collar and white-collar classes, and this success encourages further aspirations for even greater advancement. By the same token, downward mobility can be thought of in the context of Durkheim's economic disaster, which supposedly produces psychological anomie. Available findings on anomia in relation to social mobility, both up- and downward, are ambiguous. It seems that among upper-class people, the upwardly mobile manifest a greater degree of anomia than both the stationary and the downwardly mobile, but in the lower classes, the stationary and the downwardly mobile tend to be more anomic by Srole's measure.

Durkheim has held that poverty is an effective preventive of anomie, because it teaches men to restrain themselves; this would apply especially in countries where poverty is the rule, the acquisitive philosophy of capitalism is not pervasive, and class differences are accepted as the natural order. In a modern industrial society, however, such as the United States, which is rich, capitalistic, and egalitarian, poverty may have the opposite effect. It acts as a hindrance to achieving ever-increasing prosperity, which is commonly accepted as a desirable goal. This is essentially Merton's position. Consequently, according to this view, poor people in the United States might be expected to be more anomic than their richer compatriots. By the same reasoning, other classes of disadvantaged people, e.g., the uneducated, the old, minority groups, holders of prestigeless occupations, would similarly be expected to be anomic. There is indeed some evidence that income, age, ethnic minority status, occupational prestige, and education are related to anomia in the manner indicated. These relationships, however, are rather weak, and sometimes inconsistent. Particularly where occupational prestige and education are concerned, their effect on anomia at times would appear to depend on other factors, such as race (black or white), or the rural-urban distinction.

It follows as a consequence of Merton's revised view of anomie in the modern context that upward social mobility (improving one's lot) means closing, or at any rate narrowing, the gap between the acquisitive goal and the means of attaining it, and downward mobility has the opposite implication. This means that upward, in comparison with downward, mobility is less conducive to anomic conditions. This conclusion, it is to be noted, is at odds with the one derived from Durkheim's view of anomie, which was that both kinds of social mobility upset the balance of the norms governing aspirations and opportunities. It was shown earlier that the little bit of available evidence does not support this latter hypothesis. Nor, as it turns out, is it in keeping with the revised estimate of how social mobility affects psychological anomie, if this is measured by Srole's anomia. In both cases, the influence of mobility on anomie seems to be mediated by the initial social class of the person who moves.

Again, according to Merton's conception, suicide is only an extreme form of reaction to anomie. Among the milder reactions is what might be called withdrawal from social participation, or isolation. This would mean that anomic persons are less likely to participate in formal and informal associations, and, obversely, those who are active in such associations, especially the leaders, are less apt to be anomic in the psychological sense. In terms of the measure of anomie under consideration, there is some evidence supportive of both these propositions.

To recapitulate: It has been argued that we have no way of showing directly that the psychological component of anomie as conceived by Durkheim or Merton is measured by Srole's scale called anomia, because there are no objective criteria for the former. Existing sociological findings have been surveyed to determine if persons subjected to conditions that are supposed to be causally related to anomie are discriminated by the anomia scale; this would have given us indirect evidence that Srole successfully measures anomie. Here it was found that persons who are expected to be anomic by theory are by and large measured to be so by the anomia scale, although there are findings that do not clearly support the validity of this scale, even some that seem to vitiate it. The question now to be raised is: Does this add up to validating the claim that Srole's scale measures the psychological component of anomie?

5.

It appears that the anomia scale may not be unique in bearing the kinds of relationship it does to the supposed conditions of anomie. As for making verbal sense, it is possible to construct a scale consisting of statements that are obviously more indicative of the verbal construct called anomie. Take, for example, the following statements:

1. With everything in such a state of disorder, it's hard for a person to know where he stands from one day to the next.
2. Everything changes so quickly these days that I often have trouble deciding which are the right rules to follow.
3. I often feel awkward and out of place.

These would appear to reflect the notion of normlessness and the feeling of uneasiness, supposed correlates of anomie, as well as, if not better than, Srole's statements.

As a matter of fact, a scale has been constructed out of these and six other similar statements, none of which were taken from Srole; this scale is called "Anomy" by its originators, McCloskey and Schaar. This measure is of a relatively recent origin and, consequently, studies attesting to its validity are meager. But the inventors of the scale claim that it is related to income, age, marital status, occupational status, ethnic status, mobility, education, and urbanization, in the manner to be expected from speculations about anomie, as was Srole's anomia to most of these factors. Moreover, where income and education are concerned, for which the strength of relationship has been calculated for both scales, the Anomy scale might be considered superior to anomia. There are also other scales which are constructed from different statements and are supposed to measure other social psychological dimensions, such as ethnocentrism and authoritarianism, but these relate to the anomia scale as if they all measure the same thing. In fact, there is at least one study which shows that all these scales together measure one continuum, whatever it may be called. Thus it is not clear whether anomia alone measures the psychological state of anomie and, what is more, whether it measures something else which other, differently named scales also measure.

It is not even necessary to go to artificially constructed scales to find measures that parallel Srole's anomia in their relationships to more objective factors that are thought to be associated with anomie, such as income, age, and occupational and ethnic status. For example, education, or a lack thereof, as measured by the number of years of schooling completed, relates to these factors much as anomia does. That is, the less schooling a person has, the more likely is it that he is old, earns little money, holds an unprestigious occupation, and belongs to an ethnic minority in terms of race, nationality, or cultural background. Furthermore, each of these factors, according to available studies, is more strongly related to education than to anomia. Thus, if we were to predict these characteristics we would be much better off using education as a predictor than anomia.

Why, then, it might be asked, do sociologists need Srole's anomia scale when it does not predict any better than education, which has the practical advantage of measuring something that we can all readily identify and is easy to measure? Or, even more fundamentally, why do we need the concept of anomie itself, which we can measure only incompletely and can relate to empirical facts only imperfectly? Most sociologists would undoubtedly respond to the second question: "We need anomie as an explanatory concept." And to the first: "We must measure anomie to verify empirically the explanations involving this concept." Having postulated the necessity to measure anomie, we proceed to measure it and then to validate it. But the question of the validity of anomia would have not arisen, had we not felt compelled to measure anomie, had we not thought this concept useful for explanatory purposes. Why do we find this concept useful?

The only apparent reason is that *it appeals to our common sense cosmology.* We all accept the dictum that a man in despair would commit suicide. Where we would not be content with the demonstration that the objective condition of a "norm vacuum" leads to suicide, we are soothed into nodding comprehension when the notions of despair, anxiety, and unhappiness are invoked as a mediating principle. These concepts usually put a stop to the succession of whys. Practically all concepts that modern sociologists propose for explanatory purposes share this characteristic of appealing to our feelings as the irreducible elements. Like anomie, they all lead to fruitless questions of validity, for feelings are not objective and are not quantifiable.

XII. Inferential Concepts and Operations

A THEORY may contain concepts that do not refer to observable things or events. These are called *inferential*, or theoretical, concepts. It is the presence of these concepts which makes it impossible to verify a theory statement-by-statement, a characteristic of scientific theory discussed earlier. Inferential concepts are employed in scientific theories as explanatory principles, and their validity is established by checking the empirical consequences of the explanatory scheme afforded by them. There are of course other concepts in a scientific theory that are specified by measurement, such as distance and time, and are related to inferential concepts through explicit assumptions. Without these measurable concepts science as we know it would be impossible. But measurement is not extended to inferential concepts; that is, these are not directly measured. Any attempt to subject a theoretical concept to measurement results in pseudo-measurement, which is irrelevant to the task of verification.

In sociology, despite the fact that its explanations are usually formulated on a very general plane and the key concepts often refer to subjective states not open to observation, the methodological significance of inferential concepts is poorly understood. A concept such as the psychological component of anomie, which is essentially inferential, is cast in the framework of measurement, with the result that the connection between the concept and observation is rendered tenuous, as was seen in the preceding chapter. The practice of measuring theoretical concepts has even been codified into a procedural rule in sociology and thus been given methodological rationalization.

Before turning to a discussion of this sociological practice, which is the objective of this final chapter, I present below a quantitative version of the kinetic theory in order to put in relief the conceptual elements of the theory that are inferential against those that are measurable, and to trace the steps by which the former are linked to the latter. The kinetic theory, aspects of which were discussed in the beginning three chapters of this book, is well suited for the purpose, since it is a successful example of a physical theory embodying easily grasped ideas, which conforms to the philosopher's idea of how a theory should behave. The task of sorting out the relevant conceptual and logical elements is made considerably easier by the formal device of resorting to symbols and mathematical equations, which in this case are within easy reach of anyone with a modicum of high school algebra. The following rendition of the kinetic theory, therefore, also serves the incidental purpose of giving a glimpse of formal apparatus in a by-now-familiar theory, which can be compared with the sociological example presented earlier (Chapter VIII).

1.

The behavior of gases is explained by making certain assumptions about the hypothetical gas molecules, assumptions that are expressions of Newton's laws of motion applied to molecules. The assumed motion of the molecules is then related to observable characteristics of gases. (In the following presentation, the more important statements will be tagged with numerals in brackets for later reference.)

For convenience in deriving the relevant hypothesis it is first assumed that a sample of gas is enclosed in a rectangular container [1]. (Since the pressure of gas on the container is not affected by the shape, this assumption makes no difference in the argument to follow.) It is then assumed that molecules are submicroscopic balls that are perfectly elastic, and of equal size and mass [2]. When a molecule hits the inside of one of the walls of the container, to be represented by W, which we assume for now to be at a right angle to the motion of the molecule [3], its momentum, M, is

$$M = m|v|,$$ [4]

where m is the mass and $|v|$ the speed (absolute velocity) of the molecule (see Chapter II). Because of its perfect elasticity, the molecule bounces back from the wall with equal momentum in the opposite direction [5]. Thus the momentum of molecule per collision with the wall is $2m|v|$.

How much momentum does the molecule receive per second by this process? A molecule that is bounced off the wall, W, travels to the opposite wall and is again bounced back to W. Let us say that the distance between the wall, W, and its opposite wall is D. The back and forth distance is then 2D. How long does it take for the molecule to travel this distance? The answer is $2D/|v|$. To turn the question around: How many times does the molecule make the round trip per second? The answer is $1/2D/|v|$, or $|v|/2D$ times. Since the wall gets hit by the molecule once per round trip of the molecule and the momentum of the molecule per collision is $2m|v|$, the total momentum that the molecule imparts to the wall, W, in a second is $(|v|/2D)(2m|v|)$, or mv^2/D. But this is assuming that the molecule always travels perpendicularly to the wall, W. Obviously, a molecule must also sometimes travel obliquely to the wall. In general, then, the squared speed of a molecule, v^2, with respect to the wall, W, must be thought of as a component of the actual squared speed of the molecule, v^2 [6], which is $v^2/3$ [7]. If the average squared speed of the molecule is $\overline{v}^2$, then this component, $\overline{v}^2$, is:

$$\overline{v}^2 = \overline{v}^2/3,$$

where the bars over the squared speeds indicate averages. Thus the average per second momentum on the wall, W, is $m\overline{v}^2/3D$.

How much force is exerted on the wall? The average force, F, on the wall is simply the total momentum supplied by the molecules (per second) in the container [8]. If there are N molecules in the container, each of which has the same average momentum, $m\bar{v}^2/3D$,

$$F = Nm\bar{v}^2/3D.$$

But the force, F, is also equal to the area, A, of the wall, W, times pressure, or

$$F = PA. \qquad [9]$$

Thus,

$$PA = Nm\bar{v}^2/3D. \qquad [10]$$

D (the wall-to-wall distance) is the dimension of the container which is perpendicular to the wall, W. If the area of this wall is A, then AD is the volume, V, of this container, or

$$AD = V. \qquad [11]$$

Rewriting [10]

$$PAD = Nm\bar{v}^2/3,$$

or

$$PV = Nm\bar{v}^2/3. \qquad [12]$$

The total kinetic energy, E_k, of all the molecules due to translational (straight line) motion of the molecules is (see Chapter II):

$$E_k = Nm\bar{v}^2/2, \qquad [13]$$

and is not affected by the collisions of the molecules because of their perfect elasticity.

Hence

$$PV = (2/3)E_k. \qquad [14]$$

Now if we assume that the temperature of the gas (measured in the absolute scale), T, is proportional to the total translational kinetic energy, namely,

$$T = cE_k, \qquad [15]$$

c being some constant, it follows that

$$PV = (2/3c)T. \qquad [16]$$

If T is kept constant, the whole right-hand side of equation [16] remains constant, and therefore

$$PV = \text{constant}, \qquad [17]$$

which is Boyle's Law.

In the above derivation, statements [1], [2], [3], [6], and [15] are assumptions in the kinetic theory of gases that make possible the derivation of the hypothesis, namely, Boyle's Law. Statement

[15] is one of the basic assumptions in the kinetic theory, and it helps explain diverse phenomena in physical chemistry. Statements [4], [7], [9], [11], and [13] are definitions in classical physics. Statements [5] and [8] are both consequences of Newton's Second and Third Laws. And, finally, equation [17] relates molecules to observational data via pressure (P), volume (V), and temperature (T), which are measured operationally on a sample of gas by suitable instruments. (The rest of the expressions, namely [10], [12], [14], [16], are connecting statements leading to this final deduction.)

We can think of this bit of deduction leading to Boyle's Law as a *prediction*, which is confirmed by experimental findings. And this might be said to show the validity of the kinetic theory of matter, especially that portion which has to do with the behavior of gases. It is then clear that for this purpose the measurements of pressure, volume, and temperature (in order to keep it constant), are essential. It is equally clear that no measurements are made on molecules directly. Molecules are instead related to data through elaborate assumptions that presuppose established physical laws. These laws, however, are stated in terms of basic concepts of classical physics, namely, distance, time (in expressing speed), and mass, which in the final analysis are operationally generated. Thus, though molecules are not directly given operational expressions, they are related to empirical data through basic operations in physics.

The above presentation of the kinetic theory should not be construed as setting up a standard of theoretical sophistication to which today's sociology should be invidiously compared. It is a singularly well-constructed theory that functions admirably within the confines of classical physics; comparable accomplishments are not often encountered in other sciences, in biology, for example. But it furnishes a particularly good heuristic example of a theoretical concept, namely, molecules, and how it is utilized in a scientific theory of empirical relevance, which has been the overriding concern of this essay. It is this aspect of the theory which should provide the moral for sociology.

The import of the kinetic theory might be misinterpreted in another sense. The way the theory was presented, it begins with the concept of molecules, which are unobservable, and ends up with measured concepts, via a chain of assumptions. This might create the impression that science proceeds from a conception of intangible things, which is eventually linked to measurement. But clearly the measurements of temperature, volume, and pressure historically preceded the concept of molecules; it might even be said that the concept of molecules emerged from the observed regularities among the measured concepts. To think that the measurement of temperature, volume, and pressure were invented to give an empirical content to the notion of molecules would be a gross distortion of the relationship between measurement and theoretical concepts. And yet, *it is precisely this kind of upside-down procedure that prevails in current sociology,* as I will try to show in the following paragraphs.

2.

The so-called intervening variable in sociology is in essence an inferential concept. This fact was clearly recognized by Edward Tolman who introduced the label and made it popular in psychology about thirty years ago; he went so far as to say that a theory is a set of intervening variables. As the adjective "intervening" implies, these concepts are imagined to mediate between two events or things in a causal nexus and they often refer to subjective states of a person. The explanatory concepts in sociology that were encountered earlier, such as "relative deprivation" and "status inconsistency" (in Chapter VIII), as well as "anomie" (in Chapter XI), have been interpreted as intervening variables embodying these characteristics. Furthermore, the word "variable" suggests something that can assume numerical values, and accordingly intervening variables are thought of as objects of measurement. The attempts to measure anomie discussed in the preceding chapter illustrate this point.

The practice of "measuring" inferential concepts in sociology appears to stem from a misconception about a methodological policy sometimes called "operationism." At one time, this policy was understood to mean, rightly or wrongly, that every concept in a scientific discourse must be defined or specified as to its meaning by reference to the operations that could be performed. The concept of length, for example, is "defined" by referring to the procedure by which we use the yard stick in the case of medium-sized objects, or the surveyor's theodolite in the case of measuring large pieces of land by triangulation. It was thought that other concepts in a scientific theory were to be similarly measured. It is interesting to note that this form of operationism roughly coincided with or slightly preceded the currency of intervening variables, and it was probably not an accident that the latter concepts were thought to be something that should be measured. In the meantime, there has been a revision, or actually a clarification, of the operationist's position, which recognizes the importance of inferential concepts that are not directly observable and, therfore, not measurable. The concept of molecules is an example in point. The original naive operationist's view, however, seems to have lingered on in psychology for a while, then later also in sociology, producing the practice of putting an operational facade on inferential and other unmeasurable concepts.

An attempt was made recently in sociology to promote and justify the use of intervening variables by Paul Lazarsfeld, a man who has contributed much to modern empirical sociology in terms of both substance and method. His purpose was to show how inferential concepts, including intervening variables, are measured and to suggest the rationale for the procedure. Lazarsfeld describes a typical route by which an inferential concept is born and given numerical expression, and thus makes explicit a procedure subscribed to by most practicing sociologists. First, in trying to explain observed regularities, a sociologist conceives a vague "image," or a construct, that seems to underlie the phenomenon to be explained. For example, the meaning that a per-

son attaches to the concrete situations in which he finds himself
might be singled out as the explanatory factor. It might be
thought to link a man's belief system to his mode of behavior, as
Max Weber in effect did (see Chapter VI). This initial imagery
is usually taken from the vocabulary of everyday language. Second, the sociologist then sharpens this vague concept by analyzing it into components, or dimensions. The notion of meaning
that a man gives to the situation, for example, may be separated
into the four pattern variable components, as was outlined in
Chapter VI. The pattern variables are, as will be recalled,
"universalism-particularism," "affectivity-affective neutrality,"
"diffuseness-specificity," and "quality-performance."

The third, and crucial, step is to "measure" one or more of the
analytically separated components of the concept, depending
on the interest of the sociologist, for the purpose of discriminating (and classifying) the objects of the investigation. For sociologists these are individuals or collectivities such as families,
cities, hospitals, countries, etc. How do we measure, for example, the pattern variable of universalism-particularism? Let us
suppose that we decide to measure this as a psychological disposition of a person. We might then be able to find out the individual propensity to act universalistically or particularistically
by observing how he reacts to a hypothetical situation of the following kind: "You are riding with a friend who drives through a
stop sign and causes damage to another car. You are the only
witness besides the other party involved in the accident and are
asked to testify in court. If your friend asks you to lie for him,
would you do it?" The description of the situation could, of
course, be made more detailed, depending on the investigative
circumstances, though perhaps all the contingencies could never
be spelled out to make the situation completely determinate for
every potential respondent. (This is a difficulty that accompanies
the questionnaire/interview method of data collection, especially one that uses hypothetical questions.) At any rate, it is reasonable to assume that a person who has a tendency to interpret

a situation in a particularistic fashion is more likely to answer this question affirmatively than one who is universalistically inclined. But obviously this is not the only criterion of particularism, since there are other reasonable questions of the same type that we can ask. For example: "If you know your friend committed murder, would you testify falsely on his behalf?" Now, if a man says "yes" to one but "no" to the other, is he particularistic or not? It depends on which of the two situations is more indicative of the particularistic orientation. For this reason, the answers to these hypothetical questions are called indicators. An indicator is thought to measure an inferential concept only imperfectly, some more so than others.

But this way of looking at the relationship between a hypothetical construct and empirical data immediately raises two questions. One, how do we know what indicators are reasonable? And, two, is there a limit to such indicators for any inferential concept? The answer to the first question is "common sense," much as we dislike admitting it. And the answer to the second is "no." This being the case, an inferential concept is always only partially tapped for its meaning, and consequently when its relationship to another concept revealed by the indicators is contrary to what might be expected from a theory, we cannot reject the theory. Indicators thus serve as a convenient device for holding on to our favorite theories.

The fourth step in relating an inferential concept to the observational level, according to Lazarsfeld, is to combine the indicators into an index or indices. One method of accomplishing this is Guttman's scalogram analysis, which was briefly explained in the preceding chapter. For instance, the reactions of different groups of people to hypothetical questions supposedly involving the pattern variable choice of universalism and particularism have been shown to form a Guttman scale. Similar results have been obtained for the other pattern variables. There are other methods that essentially combine indicators into indices, although the process involved may not always be construed as combining indicators or producing indices. (These methods will not be described here, for an attempt to do so would take this discussion too far afield.)

One advantage of an index over an indicator is that it shows whether indicators seemingly measuring the same inferential concept "hang together" by some technical criteria, such as that they should define a continuum in the Guttman sense. In the process, indicators that do not "fit" can also be weeded out. Another advantage is that it discriminates individuals (or collectivities) more finely than single indicators, leading to a more detailed characterization and classification. But obviously an index still measures only part of the concept or a component thereof, if any at all, and the technical criteria of index construction in no way guarantee that the index measures the inferential concept. It simply shows that the indicators making up an index tap different points on a dimension, but as to whether the dimension is the same thing as the initial vague image is left to our "reasonable" assumption. In this respect, an index has the same problems as an indicator.

3.

In an apparent attempt to solve these problems, Lazarsfeld has formulated an intriguing hypothesis in the form of a doctrine, or a rule, which he calls the "interchangeability of indices." The rule states, in effect, that if there is a set of "reasonable" indicators for an inferential concept, two (or presumably more) indices formed out of subsets of these indicators will relate to another variable in essentially the same manner. (This rule, judging from Lazarsfeld's argument, seems to apply to indicators as well.) It does not hinge on a mutual correlation between the indices, but on the similarity between the ways in which they relate to another variable, possibly an indicator or an index of a different inferential concept.

Lazarsfeld is explicit about this point. For example, in a study that he cites in support of his argument, the indices of social class do not parallel each other; the people whom one index classifies as "upper class" are not necessarily so classified by the other. But it is alleged that they relate to the attitude toward labor issues, "measured" by a series of indicators, in a similar manner; people who are classified as "upper class" by either method tend to respond to labor issue questions in more or less the same fashion; and the same goes for the "lower class" people. Thus, one of the ways by which an index (or an indicator) can be judged to measure a concept is to see if it relates to some relevant phenomenon in much the same manner as another index of the same concept.

But Lazarsfeld has not produced a convincing demonstration of this principle. As a matter of fact, the example that he adduces shows flaws in his argument. The indices of social class in the above example are related to each other with a coefficient of .68, which might be considered better than the average in sociological research (the maximum absolute value of the correlation coefficient, which is attained when two variables are very closely related to each other, is 1.0, and the minimum, 0.0). When these indices are related to the attitude indicators 102 times (seventeen indicators used in six different geographical regions), yielding 102 pairs of correlations, it is found that in over 50 per cent of these correlation pairs close agreements are observed; agreements of lower degrees are also observed among the rest.

What is overlooked, however, is the fact that this incidence of agreement is just about what might be expected if, and perhaps only if, the relationship between the indices is in the neighborhood of .68 to begin with. The principle that the mutual intercorrelation between two indices of an inferential concept is independent of the relationship between each index and another variable is important in Lazarsfeld's scheme for establishing the validity of indices which are empirically not related to one another, instances of which are many in sociology. Thus, unless this principle can be demonstrated more convincingly, both theoretically and empirically, we cannot ignore the mutual relation-

ship between indices in evaluating their purported relationship
to the underlying concept.

The example of the two social class indices has another aspect
that exposes the weakness in the foundation of the doctrine of
interchangeable indices. In the great majority of the cases—93
per cent, to be exact—the correlation between either index of
social class and the attitude indicators is very low, being less
than .30. This means that the relationship between a man's class
position as measured by either index to an attitude indicator is
so tenuous that, if we were to guess his response to an attitude
question by the social class index, we would be wrong about 90
per cent of the time or more where 93 per cent of the questions
are concerned. An index that has such a low power of empirically predicting the "attitude toward labor" is practically
useless as far as this latter variable is concerned. What is more
important, it would not be difficult to invent other indices, at
random, irrespective of their presumed relationship to social
class, that correlate with the attitude indicators to the same low
degree. To put it another way, the two social class indices agree
with each other in their lack of relationship to the attitude indicators beyond what might be expected purely as a chance phenomenon. It is difficult to see how the fact that two indices are
interchangeable in not being able to relate to a third variable
establishes that they measure the same inferential concept.

4.

In relating theoretical concepts to empirical data in sociology,
it has become rather fashionable, thanks to philosophers of science, to talk about "interpreting" the former in terms of the latter. Indicators and indices are thus thought of as interpretations
of theoretical concepts. This expression came about because of
the difficulties that philosophers have had in giving a satisfactory account of how the abstract edifice of science is related to
the concrete. It was found that this relationship could not be
fully expressed in the context of definition, that is, by saying that

the concrete defines the abstract, in the traditional sense, or in terms of what are technically known as reduction sentences, in which the former gives the sufficient and necessary conditions for the latter.

Despite the suggestiveness of the expression "interpretation" and the colorful metaphors that sometimes accompany it, the philosophers have so far failed to give us the logical structure of interpretation or the rule that governs scientifically effective interpretations. For instance, equating P and V in the expression, $PV = $ constant, with measures of, respectively, the pressure and volume of a sample of gas is referred to as an interpretation. But so is associating dreams or slips of the tongue with certain psychoanalytical concepts, without much differentiation. This practice has created an unfortunate impression in sociology that concepts, no matter how vague, somehow have an ontological status independent of, and antecedent to, our sense experiences and that the observables, for example indicators, are shadows which reveal, though never fully, the ideal being. As long as concepts are thought to have an existence independent of measuring operations, as long as operations only partially interpret those concepts, especially if we are willing to accept a low level of empirical accountability, any pet ideas of ours would survive with a reasonable assurance, provided that they are professionally fashionable. Thus the survival of common sense conceptual schemes in sociology today, which continue to hold back the development of sociology as a science, is due to this view of measuring operations in relation to theoretical concepts.

The notion of interpretation is useful for the one-sided purpose of analyzing the structure of highly developed sciences from a logical point of view, rather than for tracing or otherwise accounting for how observations get organized and generalized into abstractions. This bias is too easily forgotten by sociologists who are anxious to rank sociology with the sciences. But the relationship between a theoretical concept and the observables can be seen from the point of view of the process by which the concepts are formulated as well as from the angle of a logician analyzing an accomplished science, for example physics. The former approach would actually appear to be more appropriate for sociology today, which has yet to discover a quantitative generalization that can be called a law, let alone an axiomatic theory.

From the vantage point of building up a science, it is useful, and perhaps historically valid, to view the more basic theoretical concepts of a science as generalizations of particulars, or specific operations leading to the discovery of quantities. The notion of length, or distance, for example, is generated by the operations of measuring—such as, by directly comparing objects side by side, by stepping off with feet, by triangulation, by a yard stick, etc. Equating a line segment in geometry to a physical distance between, say, two houses may be considered an interpretation of a theoretical concept, but equally the former can be thought of as a generalization of the latter and other measurements between two physical objects. It is customary to think of geometry as an abstract system with an existence of its own, but it is just as reasonable to say that it is an empirical science that has only one basic concept, distance, which is based on empirical operations of measuring length.

Viewing operations as generating concepts, instead of the other way around, places primitive operations—operations that are simple to perform and whose significance derives from daily usage rather than from other operations and concepts—at the foundation of a science. The ultimate test in science is predicated on the sense judgment of men and the perceptual consensus among them, and the concepts figuring at this level of scientific activity can only derive their meaning from operations of common usage. For example, without the concept of length many of the explanations in physics are not possible, and the meaning of this concept initially comes directly from the common practices of measuring, which we call collectively length measurement.

The difficult problem of what operations can be regarded as measuring the same thing cannot be elaborated upon here. This question, as a variant of a more general one, "what is sameness?," probably does not have a satisfactory answer. Within the scientific context, however, practice delimits the criteria of sameness, depending on the level of precision desired. If a common sense level prediction (or validation) is all that is required, operations roughly judged to produce similar results can be lumped together. But a more precise prediction (or more exacting validation) must rely on more systematic evidence, such as that afforded by quantification in the sense defined in Chapter IX. In either case, the final criterion is the commonality of every-day practice.

A policy for sociology as a beginning science suggested by these considerations is to direct our attention to concepts inti-mately tied to simple quantitative operations that are easy and require little or no technical elaboration by virtue of being part of our daily practices. Of course, not all such operations will turn out to have explanatory import. But this can only be found out by trying. Any scientific theory of substance must also con-tain derived concepts, including inferential ones, which are removed from the primitive operations (for example, pressure, density, and, of course, molecules, in physics), but these must be defined in terms of the operationally primitive concepts.

At any rate, it is unrealistic to think that a set of theoretical concepts can be defined, operationally or otherwise, in a whole-sale fashion, and that they will give us a global explanation of social phenomena. It would appear that, at the beginning, the scientific utility of a concept will have to be pegged to laws that account for only a segment of the social world. Such laws can be very general, though not explaining many different kinds of so-cial phenomena. For example, Galileo's law of motion is gen-eral in the sense that it applies to all motions, but is limited in scope in relating to heat or electromagnetism. Judging from the experience of other sciences, simple quantitative operations that are capable of generating basic sociological concepts are proba-bly not many, not more than a few. But a well-chosen few can generate many derived concepts. It is also possible that we should not rule out what we consider to be physical concepts, such as distance and time, as part of the basic sociological vocabulary. If human behavior is part of nature, it is not unlikely that some of the concepts that have proved useful in other sciences will enter in the basic principles of sociology.

This is, of course, not to detract from the potential use of the measuring techniques developed or adopted in sociology in recent years, such as Guttman scalogram analysis. But the utility of measurement lies not in presuming it to be a shadow of a vaguely conceived idea, but in relating it to other operationally defined concepts. To go back to the example of the pattern variables, these supposed components of behavior have been "measured" and even been "validated" by showing that they are related to other empirical interpretations of the pattern variables. But since it is unclear what the pattern variables denote in empirical terms, it is not certain whether the "measures" are really of the pattern variables. It might be more constructive, in the long run, to take these indices, if they are to be used at all, as unknown quantities and to discover their meaning by relating them to other operationally defined concepts.

The meaning of an operationally defined concept lies only in how it relates to other concepts, and strictly speaking the name that it bears is completely irrelevant. If a concept generated by determinate operations is a viable one, it will foster a large number of empirical relationships, all of which will contribute to the shaping of its meaning. The meaning of an operationally defined concept is not in the name but in the empirical laws in which it is used, empirical laws that make up a theory of the observable world. The significance of operations in building up a science of sociology is, thus, not that they give interpretative expressions for preconceived ideas but rather that they should beget basic concepts that can be worked into empirically valid sociological theories.

The operational policy suggested here does not deny the role of an intuitive hunch in science. But the value of a hunch is not in being interpreted as a series of indices that have tenuous connections with the inspired guess, but in leading the scientist to operations that will bear fruitful concepts. *The basic quantitative concepts that will change sociology from a pre-science to a science have not yet been discovered and await a man with a big hunch.*

EPILOGUE

1.

Modern sociologists have set up science as the model for sociology. They have, however, viewed science as proceeding primarily from the abstract to the concrete, from concepts to facts, and have neglected the reverse aspect, going from observation to generalization. This one-sided conception of science has been evident not only in the theoretical aspects of sociology but also in its empirical practices and has perpetuated a conceptual framework tied to common sense cosmology, which in turn has arrested the development of sociology as a science.

The logical structure of scientific explanation is deductive. But this characteristic, which has recently been seized upon by the more theoretically minded sociologists, is discernible, if only vaguely, also in common sense explanations. Thus the validity of scientific explanation does not depend on its deductive structure alone; it derives more from empirical verification, which means checking observable consequences of an explanation, or predictions, against facts. This is the significance of prediction in science. The utility of science is also tied to this empirical aspect, for a theory that can correctly predict natural events can be made to work for the good of man as well. Utility, however, is not a sufficient ground for fostering scientific enterprise, judging from history. Indeed, preoccupation with practical benefits, especially during the formative stages of a science, puts a restraint on the free play of the imagination and thereby stunts scientific growth. Utilitarianism is limiting in this context because an intellectual activity geared to man's practical goals is likely to be molded by the conceptual framework within which the goals are set. The pre-scientific conceptual frame of reference is that of common sense, which views the world as if it were man-made and imputes human-like motives to natural events. From this point of view, common sense explanations are animistic; so was the Aristotelian cosmology. The trouble with animism is not so much that it puts man in the center of the universe as that it appeals to the introspective understanding of men as the meaningful criterion of valid explanation. Modern science was born by breaking this conceptual mold during the Scientific Revolution. But it has been more difficult to eradicate the same mental outlook in the study of man, and the vestiges of animism linger on in sociology.

Max Weber, a prominent figure in the history of modern sociology, squarely puts our intuitive understanding at the center of his methodology; the sociology that he founded and which prospers today has in fact been called "sociology of understanding." The basic tenet of the Weberian sociology is that a man's behavior is governed by his evaluation of the situation he finds himself in, the evaluation being predicated upon goals and means. The connection between a man's situational evaluation and his action is established by introspecting how we would behave in similar situations. In his famous explanation of the rise of capitalism, for instance, he argues persuasively that Protestantism, especially its Puritanical elements, taught believers to work hard and continuously as a Christian duty and to abstain from worldly pleasures, and that capitalism is characterized by the rational organization of economic activity and accumulation of capital. It is "understandable," Weber in effect maintains, that the Protestant norms of behavior should lead to capitalist enterprises, and thus the relationship between the two phenomena is "explained."

Quite aside from Weber's erudition, which was considerable, his mode of establishing explanatory links between phenomena of interest is a familiar technique in everyday explanations, and it is to be found at different levels of sociological analysis today. At any rate, Weber's influence has been extensive in modern sociology, his conceptual schemes having been elaborated upon and made explicit, especially in the hands of Talcott Parsons. In this later development, which articulates the purposiveness of man's behavior and the introspective foundation of sociological analysis, the common sense legacy of current sociological thinking is made very clear.

The notion of purpose occupies a more prominent position in another main tradition in modern sociology, namely functionalism. Functional analysis explains a social phenomenon by postulating that it serves the function (purpose) of contributing to the well-being of the whole (society) of which it is part. Purposes are also pervasive in common sense explanations—teleological explanations. Many a "why" question in daily discourse elicits an answer that gives a purpose as the reason. But reason giving does not always constitute an explanation in the scientific sense, and often degenerates into tautologies; purposes are often invented on the spur of the moment so that the facts to be explained can be said to serve precisely those purposes. Teleological explanations can be constructed so as to evade circularity, as has been demonstrated by cybernetics. But this is not the route that functionalism has taken in sociology. Instead, it has tended to posit vaguely specified purposes, such as social survival, which merely have intuitive appeal. The prevalence of this approach in today's sociology undoubtedly is due to an animistic heritage, which sees natural events, including social phenomena, as being caused by human-like agents whose motives can be intuited by introspection.

The Davis-Moore theory of social stratification is a good example of functional analysis in sociology. It explains the existence of social inequalities by maintaining that they serve the purpose of contributing to the proper functioning of the society. But here the fact of social stratification, the object of explanation, as well as the state of social well-being, is hazily identified and the whole exercise loses much of its scientific relevance.

This circumstance illustrates the tenuousness of sociological theories in general, not just functional analysis, that are fash-

ioned on a grand scale. The Davis-Moore theory, as an explanation of *why* social inequalities exist, not merely what effect
they produce, necessarily presupposes a postulate that social
inequalities are inevitable. The authors of this theory, however,
have been reluctant to commit themselves to this stand, with
the result that it is uncertain as to exactly what is being explained by the theory. The inevitability thesis is no doubt
unpalatable to the modern intellectual who subscribes to the
egalitarian ideal, but patently one cannot have a "why" explanation of social inequalities *and* the egalitarian ideal too. This may
seem like a conflict of values, between science and ideology. But
it is not, since the demand for an explanation of *why* social inequalities exist also stems from a bias, a world view that everything has a purpose.

The deductive structure is immanent in these sociological explanations; but it is only implicit, buried under verbal disquisi-
tions that blur the line of reasoning. The deductive aspect of
scientific explanation has captivated modern sociologists, and
theories have been constructed postulationally, that is, with explicitly stated postulates from which explanations of known facts
can be deductively obtained. Attempts have also been made to
frame theories in formal terms, using symbols and the calculus
of reasoning, namely logic and/or mathematics.

Homans' theory of social behavior is a relatively well-known
example of a postulational scheme in sociology which, however,
makes no systematic attempt to use a formal apparatus except
for occasional mathematical equations. His basic postulates are
to a large degree reformulations of principles from Skinnerian
psychology, which in the process of being recast in common
sense terminology lose their verificational edge, and hence their
scientific import. Some of these postulates, paraphrased, would
have it that a man tends to perform and repeat an activity that
is valuable to him. But unless the value of an activity can be
established by some criterion other than the fact that it is
performed frequently, this proposition generates circular explanations. Homans is aware of this danger. Nevertheless, his ex-

planations often rely on this kind of circular reasoning, which is scarcely averted by making ad hoc assumptions (e.g., preaching to the unconverted is valuable). Homans has stated openly that he wants to incorporate common sense notions as basic principles of his theory (e.g., man does what "pays"). But Homans' theory is common sense in a much more fundamental sense than that it borrows commonly accepted generalizations and uses a plain language. Its conceptual cast is essentially animistic-teleological and it utilizes familiar tricks of common sense argument, such as circularity, ad hoc assumptions, the *ceteris paribus* clause, and inconsistent definitions, all of which make it impossible to verify the theory empirically. Homans' claim to validity is plausibility—how the theory can be fitted over known facts, not how it can unambiguously lead to testable predictions.

James Davis' reconstruction of the social psychological balance theory, which is designed to account for a body of available observations and generalizations in sociology, is more formal. And yet, there are logical ellipses in the structure that prevent a consistent flow of explanations from the theory. In addition, the principle that the theory applies only if certain unspecified conditions hold is a permanent feature of this explanatory scheme, and the empirical significance of the key terms, such as "liking" and "similarity," is indeterminate, though intuitively appealing. Thus, in this theory, as in Homans', the introspective elements constitute an important device by which explanation is made to "work"; the same elements prevent the theory from being stood on its head for verificational purposes. The balance theory again conceives of human action as being directed toward a goal—to increase the net "value" of interrelationships, a goal that can best be shown to exist only after the fact.

The upshot of these considerations is that when a theory is cast in a conceptual framework that derives its basic notions and line of reasoning from folk wisdom, it cannot be made to function in a scientific context just by superimposing a postulational or formal structure over it. Homans has been criticized in sociological circles for reducing sociology to psychology. But the use of psychological principles is perhaps inevitable in a complete sociological theory, and provided that these principles are scientifically sound, a reductionist approach cannot be objected to. Nevertheless, the "psychological" elements in Homans' and Davis' theories appeal to introspection and intuition rather than leading to objective verification. The same is even more true of other sociological explanations where subjective concepts, such as situational meaning, feeling of deprivation, expectation, etc., figure without any reference to systematic psychology. This kind of psychologism without discipline is to be found at the bottom of most sociological explanations today, and it is a proper ground for criticism, for it stands in the way of sociological explanations that are not only plausible but also empirically verifiable.

The verificational requirement of science, of course, has not been entirely unheeded in sociology, at least in form. "Test of hypothesis" and "measurement" are both prominent features of modern sociology. Sociologists typically "derive hypotheses" from theories and "test" them by "measuring" relevant "variables," which are then related to each other. But since the so-called hypotheses are often obtained from vague generalities with uncertain implications by reasonable sounding arguments, the relevance of testing such hypotheses is in doubt. Furthermore, "measured variables" are often neither variables nor measurable—for example, intervening variables—with the result that the use of numbers, which passes for measurement in sociology, frequently assumes ritual significance and little more.

Numbers are eloquent, but manipulation of numbers does not necessarily constitute quantification or measurement. The use of numbers and mathematics has been important in the development of modern science, but occultism too has been served by it. The significance of quantitative concepts in science derives from the fact that they are based on empirical relationships among objects (things, events, people), relationships that display determinate characteristics. These characteristics in turn make it meaningful to assign numbers to the objects, that is, to measure. Where this empirical foundation is lacking, representing a concept in mathematical expressions, implying quantitative relationships, is misleading. Quantification is really a matter of *discovering* empirical connections of predictive and explanatory import among objects, rather than of *inventing* techniques that give numerical expressions to concepts presumed to have explanatory significance. Operations, or empirical activities, by which this discovery is made are therefore at the base of concept formation in science.

In sociology, concepts are "operationalized," or "given operational meaning." This expression betrays the prevalent view concerning the proper conduct of sociological inquiry. It is that in the beginning is the word, and the word becomes "operationally defined." But this is a fundamental misunderstanding of the place that operations occupy with respect to concepts in science, resulting in a kind of upside-down operational policy. The philosophical analysis of the scientific structure which has it that formal terms in a theory are empirically "interpreted" for explanatory and verificational purposes, has been understood to be in keeping with this mistaken policy. But the notion of interpretation has been more convenient in the context of analyzing science as a finished product than in showing the process by which scientific discoveries are made. Furthermore, it does not imply that all concepts in a scientific theory can or should be so interpreted; theoretical, or inferential, concepts clearly are not subject to operational interpretation.

The operational policy in sociology, by contrast, makes no clear distinction between inferential and measurable concepts, and treats both as objects of measurement. Thus, "anomie"—at least, the current psychological reconstruction of it—has been "measured" and hypotheses involving the concept have been "tested" using numerical data. But this practice raises the futile question of "measurement validity," for there is no empirical criterion by which an operational procedure can be judged to measure theoretical concepts. As a consequence, theories involving such concepts, for example Durkheim's thesis that anomie causes suicide, remain essentially unverified.

Paul Lazarsfeld, a preeminent methodologist in sociology today, has explicitly codified the process by which sociologists "measure" inferential concepts, or intervening variables, and has formulated a "doctrine"—"interchangeability of indices"—which is supposed to justify this practice. But an examination of the underlying rationale shows flaws in the argument. Lazarsfeld in effect condones, without sound justification, the practice of putting concepts before operation and of measuring concepts indiscriminately. Thus, *the essentially animistic cosmology of current sociological thinking has been paired with a methodology of conceptual realism, which together keep sociology in a prescientific state.*

2.

The unstated assumption underlying this essay is, of course, that sociology *can* be a science. Sociologists have argued on both sides of this question, but in the end the correctness of this assumption can only be shown by producing a science of sociology. There are, however, technical difficulties that stand in the way of realizing this goal, which have also been discussed in and out of the field. One such difficulty I might single out here, without elaborating on it, has to do with the meager opportunities for experimentation in sociology. In this respect sociology is supposed to be like astronomy. Despite the claims made for astronomy as a nonexperimental science, however, its modern development stems directly from the success with which experimental findings of terrestrial mechanics could be applied to heavenly bodies. Galileo's physics was important in establishing the Copernican hypothesis, and one of the revolutionary aspects of Galileo's physics was his use of experimentation.

There are two conditions of experimentation that are worth noting. One is the ability to control the phenomena to be investigated and the other is the ease with which a particular experiment can be repeated. Both these conditions are difficult to realize in sociology for obvious reasons. This difficulty is not an inherent aspect of sociology but a by-product of the manner in which sociology is conceived. To put it another way, if we were to take the need for experimentation seriously in the development of scientific sociology, and confine ourselves to empirical phenomena that can be manipulated at will, we might end up with a sociology that looks rather different from what we have today.

The real obstacle to sociology as a science is not technical, but *conceptual*. The fundamental premise of modern sociology, as I have tried to show in these pages, is that human behavior is volitional and that social phenomena must be understood in terms of people's goals and their orientations to them. The basic approach is at once teleological and introspective, characteristics adding up to a kind of animism embedded in the common sense way of looking at things. The explanations that issue from this matrix have two consequences, both of which discourage verification and thereby prevent the development of sociology as an empirical science. One is that the explanations proposed from the animistic point of view preempt empirical testing because they are in accord with common sense views, and the other is that the conceptual realism prevents introspective terms from being measured in the strict sense. If this analysis is correct, there cannot be scientific sociology until there is fundamental change in the way we conceive of human beings. This is, of course, a difficult task to accomplish. What is called for is nothing short of a conceptual revolution. The last stronghold of animism, which has been losing ground through a series of jolts starting with the Copernican revolution, is in the study of man, and it is not likely that the required purge will be easy to perform. But this is an essential step that must be taken if sociology is to move forward as a science.

One of the recurrent debates in sociology is whether or not the discipline can or should be "value-free." To the extent that sociology is tied to common sense views, it will not be able to extricate itself from value judgments. For one thing, people's goals and their orientations are imputed to them on the basis of the sociologist's introspective understanding—by putting himself in their shoes—which means either a projection of the majority value complex or the sociologist's individual prejudice. In either case, the analysis is from the point of view of a vested interest. Moreover, the fact that the typical verificational procedure in modern sociology tolerates a great deal of latitude means that concepts can be interpreted empirically to produce findings in keeping with the researcher's prejudice and that the evaluation of the findings can also be biased in favor of the value-laden theory. These effects can be produced without the investigator consciously seeking to distort the observational data.

There is nothing intrinsically sacred about value-free sociology, or a value-free science for that matter. Some sociologists have given up the pretense of being free of values in their investigations, and I think this stand is an essentially honest one in the context of present-day sociology. From the point of view of creating a sociology that is scientifically *and* practically more effective, however, injecting nonscientific values into sociology is bound to be self-defeating. Value-laden sociology may serve a purpose—of promoting particular social goals that are held desirable—but because of its pre-closed conceptual schemes it is prevented from entering into the verificational enterprise, which is what makes science useful in practical terms. Thus on pragmatic grounds alone, sociology should be kept free of values as much as possible. But once again the success of this program depends on breaking the conceptual mold in which present-day sociology is held captive. This is not to say, of course, that sociologists as human beings should be value-free automatons.

The value orientation of modern sociology is evident in the choice of topics for investigation and in the framework in which they are discussed. Many research problems, as well as textbook discussions, are geared to social problems and are ameliorative in treatment. The notions of "deviance" and "malfunctioning" as opposed to "normalcy" and "well-functioning" are prevalent, and imply value standards. Thus, one implication to be drawn from the requirements of scientific sociology is that many of the current sociological preoccupations must be set aside. The scientific irrelevance of many current sociological concepts can also be deduced from their scientific and practical sterility.

The point is, of course, not that we should abandon social problems and social issues; quite the contrary. If we are interested in solving some of our many urgent social problems, whatever our prejudices, we must approach the solution via a circuitous route that goes through fundamental sociological principles, which are yet to be formulated. This will take time, but hopefully there will be some satisfactory solutions in the end. The alternative is the perpetuation of a pseudo-science that leads to no clear-cut solution and merely promotes the prejudice of the liberal, middle-class intellectual that the modern sociologist is.

The conclusion to be drawn from this essay is that sociology must begin anew from a fresh conceptual framework, one that pushes intuition and introspection to the background, instead of relying on them as the substance and main criteria of sociological inquiry. It is an inherent limitation of this recommendation that a change in outlook cannot be achieved by prescription. As in all revolutions, the process of dismantling the old structure must go hand in hand with the birth of new viable elements that break up and replace the old; without these constructive elements, destruction is pointless and ineffectual. In sociology, therefore, the place to begin this process is in discovering empirical laws that are germane, valid, and general.

Such laws cannot be decreed, but must come from the fields and laboratories where working sociologists make observations and generalizations, turning intuitive hunches into tangible results. For this reason, it cannot be suggested here what empirical laws are to be formulated and even what concepts are likely to be useful in the end. These can only be uncovered in the process of carrying out the conceptual revolution. In the final analysis, the most convincing proof that something better can be done is in doing it, and no speculation can be substituted for action.

BIBLIOGRAPHY

Selected books of more or less general interest that were used directly or indirectly in the preceding pages.

Bendix, Reinhard. *Max Weber, An Intellectual Portrait.* Garden City, N.Y.: Doubleday, 1962.

Benjamin, A. Cornelius. *Operationism.* Springfield, Ill.: Charles C. Thomas, 1955.

Berger, Joseph, M. Zelditch, Jr., and B. Anderson (eds.). *Sociological Theories in Progress.* Vol. I. Boston: Houghton Mifflin, 1966.

Braithwaite, Richard B. *Scientific Explanation.* Cambridge, Eng.: Cambridge University Press, 1956.

Bridgman, Percy W. *The Logic of Modern Physics.* New York: Macmillan, 1927.

――――. *The Nature of Physical Theory.* Princeton: Princeton University Press, 1936.

――――. *Reflections of a Physicist.* New York: Philosophical Library, 1950.

Brown, Robert. *Explanation in Social Science.* Chicago: Aldine Publishing Co., 1963.

Butterfield, Herbert. *The Origin of Modern Science.* London: G. Bell and Sons, 1949.

Conant, James B. *Science and Common Sense.* New Haven: Yale University Press, 1960.

Crombie, Alistair C. *Medieval and Early Modern Science.* Vols. I and II. New York: Doubleday, 1959.

Davis, Kingsley. *Human Society.* New York: Macmillan 1952.

Di Renzo, Gordon J. (ed.). *Concepts, Theory and Explanation in Behavioral Sciences.* New York: Random House, 1966.

Durkheim, Emile. *Suicide.* Glencoe, Ill.: The Free Press, 1960.

Ellis, Brian. *Basic Concepts of Measurement.* Cambridge, Eng.: Cambridge University Press, 1966.

Feathers, Norman. *An Introduction to the Physics of Mass, Length and Time.* Edinburgh: Edinburgh University Press, 1962.

Galilei, Galileo. *Dialogue Concerning the Two Chief World Systems.* Berkeley: University of California Press, 1967.

――――. *Dialogues Concerning Two New Sciences.* New York: H. Crew and A. de Salvio, 1952.

Gerth, Hans A., and C. Wright Mills. *From Max Weber: Essays in Sociology.* New York: Oxford University Press, 1946.

Hall, A. Rupert. *The Scientific Revolution.* Boston: Beacon Press, 1966.

Hempel, Carl G. *Aspects of Scientific Explanation.* New York: The Free Press, 1965.

————. *Fundamentals of Concept Formation in Empirical Science.* Chicago: The University of Chicago Press, 1952.

Hollingshead, August B. *Elmtown's Youth.* New York: John Wiley and Sons, 1951.

Homans, George. *Social Behavior: Its Elementary Forms.* New York: Harcourt, Brace and World, 1961.

Kemble, Edwin C. *Physical Science: Its Structure and Development.* Cambridge, Mass.: M.I.T. Press, 1966.

Kuhn, Thomas S. *The Structure of Scientific Revolution.* Chicago: The University of Chicago Press, 1962.

Merton, Robert K. *Social Theory and Social Structure.* Glencoe, Ill.: The Free Press, 1957.

————, L. Broom, and L. S. Cottrell, Jr. (eds.). *Sociology Today.* New York: Basic Books, 1959.

Nagel, Ernest. *The Structure of Science.* New York: Harcourt, Brace and World, 1961.

Parsons, Talcott. *The Structure of Social Action.* Glencoe, Ill.: The Free Press, 1949.

Popper, Karl R. *The Logic of Scientific Discovery.* New York: Basic Books, 1959.

Russell, Bertrand. *The ABC of Relativity.* London: George Allen and Unwin, 1958.

————. *The Scientific Outlook.* London: George Allen and Unwin, 1931.

Skinner, B. F. *Science and Human Behavior.* New York: Macmillan, 1963.

Taton, René (ed.). *History of Science.* Vols. I–IV. New York: Basic Books, 1963.

Weber, Max. *The Protestant Ethic and the Spirit of Capitalism.* New York: Charles Scribner's Sons, 1958.

Wolf, Abraham. *A History of Science, Technology and Philosophy in the Eighteenth Century.* New York: Macmillan, 1952.

Woolf, Harry (ed.). *Quantification.* New York: Bobbs-Merrill, 1961.

INDEX